"A fascinating account of her exciting international life!"

—(Barnaby Conrad—author of thirty-two books and founder of the Santa Barbara's Writers' Conference)

"Global Girl is a fun frolic about the hilarious adventures of a young Swedish girl, who discovers life, language and love around the world."

—(Cork Millner, author of *Hollywood Be Thy Name* and *The Warner Brothers Story*.)

"Do you want to sleep with her first or shall I?" begins a rare collection of the experiences of a young Swedish girl, who longed to see the world. Through Kerstin's colorful storytelling and insightful understanding of human relationships, the reader becomes personally involved in her insatiable quest fort adventure."

—(Maxwell Dickinson, Author of *You Kin Do It Chile, Suds; Around the World on a Horse, Bandana Country, Big Lick Walking Horse.*)

"Kerstin delights and amuses the reader with tales of her experiences as a young Swedish girl venturing to foreign countries—England, France, Spain, Japan, Italy and eventually to the United States where she has lived for many years."

—(Pat Gebhard, Author of *Motives for Murder* and *George Washington Smith; Architect of the Spanish Colonial Revival.*)

Confessions of
a Swedish Girl

Confessions of a Swedish Girl

Kerstin Shirokow

iUniverse, Inc.
New York Lincoln Shanghai

Confessions of a Swedish Girl

iUniverse books may be ordered through booksellers or by contacting:

iUniverse
2021 Pine Lake Road, Suite 100
Lincoln, NE 68512
www.iuniverse.com
1-800-Authors (1-800-288-4677)

ISBN: 978-0-595-45373-3 (pbk)
ISBN: 978-0-595-89684-4 (ebk)

Printed in the United States of America

I dedicate this book to my daughter Katya, my son Mike, and my friend Bob.

Contents

Acknowledgements

Many thanks to *Jacques de Waern*, who encouraged me to write my memoirs almost twenty years ago, and whose amusing drawings have added so much to the book.

To my dear friend, writer *Daga Nyberg,* for her encouragement and never-failing faith in me.

To *Maxie Dickinson* and her writing group, who have critiqued and improved my writing, week after week.

To Anne *Lowenkopf* and *Cork Millner*, who patiently read and listened to my writings.

To *Barnaby and Mary Conrad's Writers' Conferences,* where I learned so much, and which inspired me to continue writing.

And last but not least, thanks to Bob and all my friends and relatives, who over the years have been supportive, encouraging and helpful to me in transcribing this saga of my life.

1

From Paris to Madrid

"So, do you want to sleep with her first, or shall I?"

Was I still dreaming, or did Fernando actually say that? He must have, because Antonio answered, "Why don't you have her tonight, and I'll take her tomorrow night?"

Were they talking about me? Obviously, and they must have thought that I was still asleep. Not anymore, I wasn't. I was awake all right, and scared.

How could I have been so naïve? Here I was on my way from Paris to Madrid in a car with two Spanish men, whom I had only just met, and who were now discussing, which one of them would sleep with me, *first!*

My first thought was to tell them to stop the car and run away. But how could I? We were in the middle of the French countryside and I had very little money. I didn't know anybody and I had to be in Madrid the day after tomorrow. I decided to stay in the car, pretend to be asleep and listen very carefully to what they were saying.

◆　　　◆　　　◆

The year was 1949, and I had arrived in Paris from Stockholm on my way to Madrid, where I had been hired as an English governess in a Spanish family. From Paris to Madrid I had planned to hitchhike with the vegetable trucks, which left every morning from *Les Halles* going south towards Spain.

When I told this to my French friend Marguerite, she strongly advised me against it.

"Christine," she said," don't do it. It is far too risky. Spanish families sometimes stay at the hotel where I work. Perhaps I can persuade one of them to take you along when they return to Spain. I am sure that within a week or so, someone will arrive."

"But I can't wait a week. I am hired to start my job in Madrid on the first of July, and there are only a couple of days left."

The next day Marguerite told me, that two Spaniards, Señor Gonzales and Señor Ruiz, were driving to Madrid the next day, and would be glad to take me along. But she was not happy about my going alone with two men, whom I did not know. Couldn't I wait until I could go with a family?

Generally I listened to Marguerite's advice. She was older than I, and much wiser in the ways of the world. She had lived on her own in German-occupied Paris, whereas I had lived a very sheltered life in neutral Sweden. But this time I was afraid I'd loose my job if I didn't reach Madrid on July first as arranged. So I accepted the two Spanish gentlemen's invitation. Since they hardly spoke any French, and I did, they said they were happy to have me along to interpret for them.

Fernando Gonzales was tall, handsome and about twenty-five years old. He had black wavy hair and brown glittering eyes, which I, as a blond Swede, found exotic and attractive. Antonio Ruiz was maybe forty, short and with a little black mustache. They invited Marguerite and me out for dinner to the *Folies Bergères* and seemed very proper.

The next day I left with them. Everything was fine. I translated when we stopped for lunch and dinner and they were very nice to me. Now I understood why. They expected me to be *nice* to them in return!

This was something that never had occurred to me. But what did I know about Spanish men? Or any man for that matter? Young and still a virgin at twenty-two, I could not in my wildest dreams imagine how anything like this could happen.

We arrived at the hotel for the night. They asked me to book one double and one single room. If I had not heard their discussion, I would have assumed that they would share the double and I would have the single. Now I knew differently.

I booked the rooms and ran ahead of them upstairs to the single room, where I put my suitcase and locked the door. Then I went down and told them in front of the concierge, "Señores, I heard your conversation in the car. I just want you to know, that neither one of you is going to sleep with me. Nobody ever has, and I am taking the single room!"

They were completely confused.

"I don't understand," said Fernando. "What's the matter with you? A girl like you, who travels alone all over Europe without husband, father, brother or *dueña* cannot be anything but a *comfort* girl. You asked to go with us. Haven't we been kind and generous to you? Why would we have been, if not at least *one* of us could take you to bed?"

Here the concierge interrupted.

"But you don't understand, Señores. The young lady is a *family girl*. She is completely inexperienced in every way, and she doesn't have the faintest idea, how you could have interpreted her behavior in this way."

I broke in, "In Sweden I have hitchhiked since I was fifteen years old and no one ever assumed I would sleep with him!"

After that everything went well. I took the single room and the next day we continued to Madrid. They took me to Isabel la Catolica 5, the address of the family who had hired me as a governess. There wasn't much conversation during the trip. They didn't seem exactly angry with me—more like confused and embarrassed.

Thinking about it now I wish I could say they seemed disappointed, but I'm afraid that would be somewhat immodest of me!

After a couple of days in Madrid I understood better their confusion. My teen-age student Angela was not allowed out in the street alone even during the day, and the young women one saw alone were definitely not "family girls."

Later Fernando introduced me to his fiancée, Alicia, a beautiful dark-eyed girl, who had obviously bleached her hair blond. She was a little cold toward me at first, and asked many questions about our trip from Paris to Madrid. "Which route did you take?"

"Oh, it was a lovely route, Alicia. Here, I'll show you on the map."

But before I could show her, she asked,

"Where did you spend the night? Was it comfortable? Did you sleep well?"

She obviously knew her fiancé well. Apparently my answers satisfied her, because we became good friends.

Once I asked her why she bleached her hair. She said Fernando preferred blondes. I guess I already knew that.

When I admired a blouse she was wearing, she took it off and gave it to me. I later learned, that in Spain that is considered good manners. So you have to be careful when expressing your admiration in Spain. But I was never careful about anything I said or did. From childhood on, I took risks and chances because of curiosity, naiveté and love of adventure

Like when I fell through that roof.

2

Childhood and School Years

Through the Roof

"I am shocked at how careless parents are with their children these days," said my mother to my father, as he met her at the station.

"Did you read this?"

She handed him the local newspaper, which she had read on the train from Stockholm to our hometown Eskilstuna in Sweden.

"This poor child could have gotten herself killed. I wonder who she is? I have a good mind to call her parents and tell them what I think!"

"No need to do that, my dear," said my father. "I already know who it is."

"You do? Who?"

"It's your child, dear."

And so it was.

I was seven years old and was playing with a friend on the glass ceiling of a department store. The glass ceiling was there to let in light, and was protected by a glass house. The house had one small window, presumably for repair and cleaning purposes. I found it open one day and climbed in. Before I knew what was happening, the glass shattered and I fell through, landing on the counter for underwear and stockings (*silk* stockings; the year was 1934). Had I landed one foot to the left, I would have hit the floor. The poor sales girl fainted.

Looking up, I saw my friend's frightened face through the splintered glass in the ceiling. Since the accident happened during rush hour, many people gathered around. One older gentleman gave me a two-crown silver coin and said, "That was the funniest thing I have seen in my whole life!"

Then some employees carried me up to an office, put some bandages on my legs, where the glass had cut them, and I went home.

This was the first time curiosity put me in danger, and it prefaced my adult years.

◆   ◆   ◆

My hometown Eskilstuna (population 35.000 at the time) was a small industrial town, very conventional and safe, which to me was boring and dull. Most of the men worked at the arms factory where my father was the manager. I remember how, when the factory whistle blew at five o'clock, thousands of bicycles passed our house, the workers sitting ramrod straight and looking straight ahead. Those without bikes walked, and I can still hear the sounds of their wooden clogs against the pavement. No factory workers had cars nor leather shoes in those days. Whenever I was playing at a friend's house across the street, I was admonished to leave at "five to five" to avoid crossing the street during rush hour traffic!

Hitting the Jackpot

My childhood in Eskilstuna was protected and uneventful, with the exception of two events, other than the department store incident. The first happened one day when my mother gave me five *öre* (cents) to buy a candy bar from the candy machine at the corner. When I put the coin in, to my utter astonishment and delight *all* the little doors opened; instead of getting *one* candy bar I got *forty*! As young as I was, I knew that I was supposed to take only *one* candy bar, but the temptation was too great. I took them all.

Here another problem presented itself; where could I put forty candy bars? In those days little girls wore skirts, not pants. If I pulled my skirt up and dared to show my panties, I could take all of the bars. Modesty against greed. Greed won and I ran home, exposing my panties to the world.

But one problem was left. How to get into the house without my mother or my brothers seeing me? Had my mother seen me, she would have made me return the candy bars. Had my brothers seen me, I would have had to pay them off, so as not to tell my mother. I was lucky. I managed to get up into the attic without being seen. There I stashed my loot, which lasted over a month.

◆   ◆   ◆

My parents were not pleased with all the trouble I got myself into. But when they scolded me, and asked why I couldn't be like my sister, I answered, "Aunt Elsa is always doing things that you, Mother, never dare to do! She travels abroad to such fascinating countries and sees so many interesting things! The only foreign country you have been to is England!"

"Well," said my mother, "I would never dream of traveling alone to such strange countries, as she does. It simply isn't proper."

Aunt Elsa was my mother's younger sister. She was way ahead of her time. When young ladies went to school to learn to speak French, embroider, and maybe cook French sauces to prepare for marriage, my aunt graduated at the top of her class from the Institute of Gymnastics in Stockholm. She could have her pick of positions and became a masseuse and teacher of Swedish Gymnastics, which was very popular at the time. She taught all over Europe in wealthy and aristocratic circles.

Aunt Elsa's 85th Birthday

Shortly after I hit the jackpot at the vending machine, Aunt Elsa came to visit. Her arrival was always a *happening*. She didn't *walk* into a room; she *swept* in, dressed in the latest fashion. Her hair and makeup were perfect, and she wore a wonderful perfume called *Diorissimo*, which smelled of lily of the valley. To this day, that is my favorite perfume. My mother definitely looked dowdy by comparison.

Aunt Elsa's suitcases were like geography lessons. They had stickers from most of the European capitals and many others as well; she was always full of exciting stories about her trips abroad. On this occasion she told us about her stay as a gymnastics teacher in the royal palace in Cairo, where Crown Prince Farouk of Egypt had proposed to her and she had said, "no."

"Aunt Elsa, why did you say, 'no' to becoming Queen of Egypt? Just think: we could have been nieces to the Queen of Egypt!"

My sister and I, ages ten and five, were very upset with our much-adored aunt.

The problem was that at the time Prince Farouk was twelve years old. It turns out that one day he had told her, "*Je vous aime,* (I love you) Mademoiselle Elsa. When I am older and can have a harem, I would like you to be my number one concubine." Not exactly an offer of a crown, but that was easier to say to two little girls, who had no idea of what the words *harem* and *concubine* meant. She declined his offer and continued his gymnastics lessons.

◆   ◆   ◆

"Tell us about Cairo, Aunt Elsa. Did you see the pyramids? Did you see the sphinx? Did you ride a camel?"

"Yes, I did all those things. I love Cairo and there were lots of gentlemen who asked me out. One of them was count Antonin Tolstoy. He invited me for dinner at *Mena House*, a famous hotel in the desert, near the Sphinx. We rode there on camels."

Cairo in the period between the two World Wars was an exciting place to be for a young pretty Swedish girl, particularly one with royal connections. Many young Europeans, who had grown tired of war-torn Europe, had come to Cairo to seek their fortune. Count Antonin Tolstoy was a nephew of the writer Leo Tolstoy. He was among the many Russian aristocrats, who had fled the newly created Soviet Union. Aristocrats were no longer welcome there, and all their property had been confiscated. Fortunately for Antonin, his family had prudently put their money in foreign accounts.

"Did he want to marry you, too?" I asked eagerly.

"Yes, he did. And maybe I would have, but he asked me too soon."

"What do you mean, 'too soon?'"

"Well, we were riding on camels out in the desert on our way to dinner. While we were riding along, he proposed to me. I told him: 'no,' but I wish he had waited at least until after dessert!"

Poor Antonin, what bad timing.

◆   ◆   ◆

Many, many years later, when visiting my aunt in Stockholm, I happened to knock over a little carved Egyptian stool. As I did, I noticed some writing on the bottom of the seat, which said, *"N'oubliez pas trop tôt votre ami Antonin"* (Don't forget too soon your friend Antonin).

When I showed it to my aunt she said, "Oh, dear, I never noticed it, and I have had this stool for at least fifty years!"

As for Prince Farouk, later King Farouk of Egypt, he lost his throne in 1952 and died in Rome in the late 1960's, suffering a heart attack while eating spaghetti in a restaurant. He was supposedly accompanied by one of his "concubines."

Aunt Elsa never married, though she had many suitors, some of them quite prominent. For years she would receive expensive gifts and hard-to-get tickets to important events from obviously influential people. She accepted and sometimes took me, but she never told me from whom the tickets came. She was engaged for many years to an Englishman called Bill, whose handsome portrait stood on our piano. I admired him every day, when I practiced those boring scales. One day it wasn't there anymore.

"Mother, where is uncle Bill's portrait?"

"I took it away. It doesn't belong there anymore."

"Why? I like to look at him when I practice!"

"Well, Aunt Elsa has broken off the engagement."

Later on I found out why. Bill was part of a peace organization formed after WWI. They were all young idealists, who figured that, if all borders between countries were done away with and if everybody spoke the same language, there would be no more wars.

That's why Esperanto was invented. The plan never came to pass, but Bill in his enthusiasm and to inspire others, threw away his passport, a little prematurely as it turned out. That was much too radical for my practical and down-to-earth aunt, so she broke off her engagement to him.

After Aunt Elsa retired, she traveled a great deal, mostly all over Europe to see some of her many friends, and even came to visit me in California after I moved there. She claimed that, since she had no children, she wanted to spend all her money, so that when she died, she wouldn't have one *krona* (crown) left.

When Aunt Elsa died at age ninety, it became obvious that she had miscalculated, because there was quite a handsome sum of money in her will for each of her nephews and nieces, including me. In addition, and much to my surprise, I also received the little Egyptian stool with the French inscription by Antonin.

◆   ◆   ◆

I wanted to be just like Aunt Elsa. I aspired to have as many suitors as she did and to travel to exotic countries and meet foreign people.

In my little hometown there were no foreigners, but there were foreign movies. The first one I saw was, "*Blood and Sand*," with Tyrone Power, whom I immediately fell in love with, as did my best friend. We were both ten years old.

My best friend and I wrote "Teerohne Pohver" love letters in Swedish, addressed to: Tyrone Power, Hollywood, America. We never got any answers, but that didn't discourage us. We wrote on.

One day we read in a movie magazine that he had married the French actress Annabella. We were furious! How dared he! Didn't he know that *we* loved him and, if he married at all, it should be to one of *us*! So we fired off some more letters; not love letters this time but *hate* letters to Annabella at the address: Annabella, Hollywood, America. No answer.

◆   ◆   ◆

Twelve years passed and one day, when I was sitting by the pool at a club in Madrid with my friend Ernesto, a beautiful woman walked by.

"Do you know who that is?" asked Ernesto, "That's the movie star, Annabella."

I told him the story of my "correspondence" with Annabella and Tyrone Power, and Ernesto suggested I go and tell her. At first I hesitated. What would she think? But then I thought, why not? After the letters I had written, it might be fun to meet her. And maybe her husband was with her?

So I went over, introduced myself and said, "Please excuse me for intruding, but I have something to tell you, that you might find amusing."

Confirmation Day

She looked up, a little surprised. She was beautiful, with long blond hair, an excellent figure in a bathing suit that left little to the imagination. Annabella kindly asked me to join her and I related my tales of youthful folly. She listened quietly with a little smile on her lips and when I finished, she said,

"Well, if you still want him, you can have him!"

Then she made a beautiful swan dive into the pool and swam away.

Soon after our conversation the news broke: Tyrone Power had left Annabella for the starlet Linda Christian.

When I was fourteen, I reached the age, when most Swedish youngsters are confirmed in the Lutheran Church. It is quite an important event, and that morning I had confessed my belief before the whole congregation. I was wearing a beautiful new white dress with matching white shoes. For the first time in my life I had been to the hairdresser, and I was very pleased with the way I looked.

My older brothers and sister, Aunt Elsa and some other aunts and uncles came to our home, and now we were having a very special dinner. I was the guest of honor. During dessert Mother said,

"Kerstin, listen carefully! You are now almost grown-up and therefore you can decide a few things about your life for yourself."

"Good, I don't want to eat oatmeal porridge anymore!"

For as long as I could remember, I was forced to eat oatmeal porridge everyday for lunch, because Mother believed it was good for me.

"And I don't want to take piano lessons anymore!"

For seven years I took piano lessons once a week. Now I could decide whether I wanted to continue. I did not. Our maid would now address me as *Miss* Kerstin; about that I didn't care one way or another. All that was fine, but I wondered when were they going to tell me about the important thing, which I'd been waiting for?

I finally burst out, "Today is my confirmation day, and you are supposed to tell me!"

All my life my brothers and sister and even my parents, had teased me about the fact that I looked different from everybody else in the family, mostly because of my nose. Everybody else in the family had long, straight, aristocratic-looking noses, but my nose turned up; I had a snub nose.

After reading a story about a little girl who was adopted, I came to the conclusion that I was adopted, too. It didn't bother me though; I knew my parents loved me. In fact, because I was the youngest, I was rather spoiled and thought that they loved me best, because they had *picked* me, whereas the others they had produced without choice.

When my parents didn't say anything about my adoption, I felt it was unfair. So I asked again, this time with tears in my eyes,

"So when are you going to tell me?"

"What, dear?" my father asked with concern, "Tell you what? I don't understand."

"That I am adopted!" I cried with tears streaming down my face.

"Adopted!" they both exclaimed, "Adopted? Where in the world did you get that idea? What do you mean?"

My family was totally taken aback.

"I gave birth to you in the hospital," remarked my mother.

"And I saw you there, only a few hours old," my father followed.

"We saw you coming home from the hospital, a tiny red-faced and wrinkled little thing," said my brothers and sister.

"So where in the world did you get the idea that you are adopted?" my mother and father said together.

"Well, I don't look like anybody in the family. I have a snub nose, which you have always made fun of. All of you have straight noses!"

I burst into tears again.

My father left the room, while my mother and my siblings tried to console me without much success. When my father came back, he brought with him a portrait of a great grandaunt of mine. She was unremarkable in every way, not beautiful, not even pretty. In fact, she was very plain, but the mystery was solved. I looked like her; she had a snub nose.

◆   ◆   ◆

One morning in the fall of 1939, my father came into the kitchen while I was eating breakfast. I looked up, surprised. He was dressed in his army major uniform, which he hadn't worn since he was forced to retire several years before at the age of fifty. That was when President Woodrow Wilson had declared that World War I was to be "the war to end all wars." The surprising part of Father's appearance was how excited and happy he seemed to be, wearing his uniform once again.

"Father, the war has broken out; we might be bombed and killed, and you are happy about this?" I asked.

"Yes, I am happy! For the last several years I have felt completely useless. I have tried to find a job, and I'd do anything, but nobody in this town will hire a retired army major. My retirement pension is not enough to support your mother and the four of you, so your mother is working to support us all. But she is, after all, a general's daughter and was never meant to work. She hates her job; she doesn't feel qualified, and we both know she was hired because people felt sorry for us."

Now I understood why Mother was too tired to help me with my homework, and why she often cried in the evenings.

"Mother never had to work, until I retired. But thanks to the war, I am now back on a major's full salary and have been put in charge of the Civil Air Defense. Mother is quitting her work at the end of the month."

I had never seen my father so happy.

Shortly after that day, the Germans marched into Poland and the Soviet army attacked Finland. For my family it was as if Sweden were attacked, because my father was born in Finland. Finland had been a Swedish province for centuries, during which time Russia occupied it innumerable times. In the late 1800's, it became a Russian duchy until the Soviet revolution in 1917, when Finland saw its chance to become independent. Its independence was short-lived, however. Shortly after WWII broke out, the Russians once again attacked Finland. The Swedish government chose to stay neutral, but many Swedes wanted to help Finland against our historic enemy Russia, so a Swedish Voluntary Battalion was formed, of which my older brother, an Army lieutenant, became the leader.

My father was very proud and pleased. He had tried to volunteer when the Finns fought for their independence during WWI, but was for some reason not accepted. My mother later told me that her father, a general and Chief of the Army, had prevented it, because my mother was pregnant with her first child, my oldest brother.

Airplane Spotters

After Hitler's occupation of Denmark and Norway, Sweden was thought to be next, so Sweden sent all its troops to protect its borders. High school girls and boys, including me, were trained to be airplane spotters during the summer vacations. We were sent to man observation towers, which were built in the woods all over Sweden, and taught to handle a gun for self-defense. The tour of duty lasted three months, about the length of the summer vacation.

Our job was to watch night and day for German and Allied airplanes, which flew over Swedish territory, and to telephone their nationality, type, speed, direction and air level to central stations. Then Swedish hunter planes would chase them off to prevent them from fighting each other over Swedish territory. Being far too young to realize the seriousness of the situation, I remember those summers as marvelous adventures. There were ten of us without any grown-ups to bother us, in the middle of a Swedish forest where, from the safety of our tower, we could watch bears, wolves, foxes and all kinds of birds, moving freely around during the bright summer nights! In addition to this, we were paid a soldier's salary, except I, who was paid ten cents more an hour and given a corporal's rank. (Maybe the fact that my father was head of the Civil Air Defense had something to do with that!)

◆   ◆   ◆

At the end of my summer's adventures and back in school, I followed the advice of Aunt Elsa, who had impressed upon me the importance of language learning. Between the ages of eleven and nineteen in high school, I studied eight years of German, five years of English and four years of French. My English teacher, Erik Andersson, I shall never forget.

◆   ◆   ◆

Mr. Andersson was our senior advisor and at least sixty years old, when he declared his love for me. I was seventeen. He wrote the most beautiful, hopeless love letters with a passion, which I now understand was an older man's last, glowing feelings for a young adolescent girl, but which I *then* found embarrassing and confusing.

English was my best subject. I hoped to get a scholarship in English; so, for extra credit I translated a book by Edgar Rice Burroughs into Swedish, called "The Warlord of Mars." When I was to show Mr. Andersson the manuscript of my translation, he asked me to come to his home after school, where we sat down next to each other on the sofa. He opened a page of the book and I translated. I felt it was going very well. After half an hour or so he said, "I suppose you are pleased now that this is all over?"

"Yes, I am," I said.

"But I'm not," he replied, and put his arm around me and kissed me! I was so taken aback that I didn't resist. I just let it happen.

"Don't misunderstand me," he tried to explain. "I love my wife, and I have never been unfaithful to her. But what I feel for you is something totally different. I have never experienced anything like it. Your very presence in the classroom makes me happy. When you smile, it is as if the sun is coming out. When you are absent, my whole day is ruined. You are the most beautiful thing that has happened in my life."

All I could think about was how to get out of there. What would happen, if Mrs. Andersson came home, or one of their children, and found us there on the sofa? I kept looking out the window and saw my boyfriend, Johnny, biking back and forth. He was waiting to take me out for a soda after the exam. When I finally escaped, Johnny asked why it had taken so long and if I'd passed. I simply nodded and provided no further explanation.

My once favorite English class became a nightmare. I didn't dare to look up at Mr. Andersson, and I didn't dare to look away. On every paper he returned to me, the bottom was folded over, because he'd written questions such as, "Are you upset? Are you angry? Are you worried?" followed by long declarations of love.

I was touched, and my heart ached for him, but I was frightened that some classmates might see what he had written! I also received letters from him, some of which I saved.

"My Darling,

Monday was a black day. I am ashamed that I couldn't control myself better when you came into the classroom. Forgive me! Everything has seemed so hopeless for the last few days. The days right after the break you were wonderful; radiant with something that I have come to love since over a year ago, and which I had hoped would enrich my life forever and ever. But all of a sudden my star lost its brilliance. Why? Darkness engulfed my life. Everything fell apart.

Today I saw that you had noticed my distress. You were wonderful. You hurried to my rescue, you understood me. I met a look of the kind you used to give me. Thank you! You see how my poor soul is completely in your power. It's entirely up to you, what my fate and future will be. You are so busy now with final exams and reports, so I won't ask you to write to me. All I ask is that you some-how show me that you think of me. I shall in return, whether you believe in it or not, think of you every single moment during your finals. Only please let your star shine like before with its quiet, wise and warm light, which leads me in the right direction. That's all I ask.

Yours forever,

E."

I had never received a love letter that beautiful, but it frightened me. From then on I tried to avoid Mr. Andersson as much as possible. I was the last to enter the classroom, and the first to leave. I spent every break in the girls' restroom. But one day we met in the corridor, and I couldn't run away.

"Please, you mustn't avoid me like this," he pleaded. "I can't cope with it! You must come for a walk with me, a long walk in the park. Saturday at two o'clock we'll meet at the gate. Come! Please promise that you'll be there! Don't drive me to despair! I'll never bother you again!"

The two days until Saturday were the longest in my young life. I definitely didn't want to go but, at the same time, I felt sorry for him. If I could make him happy by just going for a walk, why not? I also felt pressure, because he was my teacher; my scholarship and final grades were in his hands after all.

So we went on our walk. The day was cold and windy, and all I wanted to do was to go home. I feared that we would meet somebody who knew us in our little town where everybody knew everybody else. Luckily we escaped unnoticed, the walk proved uneventful and we parted.

A few days later I received a poem.

"To my Love,

Slowly they walked side by side in the park,

How happy he was that she finally walked at his side.

Surrounded by radiance, although she wasn't happy, she alone was the focus of his glances.

All of a sudden it was as if the sun came out, and she and the sun became one, in a magical circle that imprisoned him.

Proudly he walked on like a triumphant young graduate.

And now, when they reached point "Y" on the road to their fate, she said with a tone of finality,

'From here on, we go our separate ways. Goodbye.'

And he saw her walk happily away on the new road toward future promise. Slowly he tramped alone the old road, the old road to nowhere."

After reading his poem I wondered how he could have seen and felt so much beauty and happiness during a walk, which for me was uncomfortable and painful. Fortunately, Mr. Andersson kept his promise and never bothered me again.

At my graduation I received a dozen red roses without a card, which made my mother very curious. I also received a book of love poems in English. In it Mr. Andersson had written:

"In remembrance of your graduation and as an expression of my sincere gratitude for what you have meant in the lead role of the incomplete dream play, for which the curtain now is down. Thank you for all your goodness, understanding, patience.

You will live in my thoughts as one who has taught me to experience feelings of unimaginable euphoria and indestructible beauty.

Now life goes on, and I want this souvenir to be a testimony of my sincere congratulations, my hope that you might meet a future worthy of yourself, with outward success as well as inner peace in all of life's vicissitudes. I'll follow you from afar, and rejoice over your every success in the new world, you now are about to conquer.

Yours Gratefully,

E. "

Many years later my mother mentioned in a letter that Mr.Andersson had died. I was a little surprised that she thought to remark on it. Surely many other of my teachers had died since I left Sweden, but she had never mentioned any of them. I wondered if she might have read my diary where I also kept his letters.

Every time I visit my hometown, I put a red rose on the grave of the man, who gave me an A+ in English.

3

University of Stockholm

After I graduated from high school, I continued my studies at the University of Stockholm. Still following Aunt Elsa's advice, I chose English as my major with minors in French and Spanish.

In order to qualify for a room in the girls' dorm I had to meet three qualifications: no money, good grades and a job at the Student Union. On the first two points I qualified easily; and, after having worked as a liaison between American students who studied at the university on their GI bills, and their Swedish landladies, I finally qualified for a room at the dormitory. I felt fortunate to have one of those sought after rooms; there were only twenty of them and over three hundred girl students.

During my employment, I enjoyed meeting the American students. I dated a few of them, including Charles McFadden, who was studying Swedish Town Planning. Charles was the first black person I had ever spoken to, and I liked him well enough, but I think the fact that he was *black* made me even more interested in him. I felt that, by going out with him, I was showing the world that I was not in the least prejudiced, a topic which was highlighted by Gunnar Myrdal, sociology professor at the University of Stockholm, who had just published *An American Dilemma,* severely criticizing the treatment of blacks in the U.S.

I invited Charles to my parents' home in Eskilstuna, telling them only that I was a bringing home an American student, something I had done many times before. In a conscious decision to emphasize to them how completely unprejudiced I was, I decided not to mention that he was black.

My parents had never seen nor spoken to a black person before; so, when they opened the door and saw Charles, they were speechless. But after the first shock of his appearance, they welcomed him, and my mother, who spoke good English, made an effort to make him feel at home.

The next morning we all went on our regular Sunday walk in the park, and there were a lot of turned heads. Charles was the first black person ever to have visited the town of Eskilstuna. Later, Charles told me something I shall never forget.

"You know, Kerstin, you are just as much prejudiced, if you go out with a person *because* he is black, as if you *don't* go out with him, because he is black."

◆   ◆   ◆

Aunt Elsa continued to impart her adventures to me.

"On the street corners in Madrid," she explained, "there are pyramids two to three meters high, consisting of hundreds of fruits, each about twice the size of a soccer ball. They are green on the outside, red on the inside with little black seeds. They are so juicy that the juice just drips down your chin, when you eat them."

I didn't believe her at first; the biggest fruit we had in Sweden was a big apple! How was I to conceptualize what a watermelon is like? Aunt Elsa also talked about many other things, which challenged my imagination: bullfights in Spain, camel rides in the Sahara, and moonlight cruises on the Danube.

I felt restricted in Sweden with all of its many rules and regulations. I was brought up, as were all young people in Sweden in the thirties and forties, not to speak to people without being introduced. One day, in an elevator with Dr. Svensson, Dentist Wickström, and Mrs. Hedberg, nobody said a word to me. They all knew that I was the Major's youngest daughter; but because we hadn't been introduced, nobody spoke. There seemed to be an endless list of things I wasn't supposed to do, because it just wasn't proper.

I didn't want to hold myself to their standards. The day when I told my parents that I wanted to get a newspaper route to make some money, they were horrified at the suggestion. That a girl from a good family would deliver papers was out of the question, as far as they were concerned.

Once when I was seventeen, my father and I were traveling from Stockholm to Eskilstuna on the train. Opposite us sat a man of about twenty-five. I was reading a newspaper and, when my father left the car to smoke, I came upon something very funny in the paper, causing me to laugh out loud. The gentleman opposite asked, "What is so funny?"

"Look at this," I said, "look at this cartoon! Isn't it hilarious?" and I went over to show it to him and we both laughed.

Just then my father came back and was obviously furious. Shortly after the young man left, he let me have it.

"How can you behave in such a cheap way? You are acting like a hussy, talking and laughing and sitting *next* to a man you don't know! Why can't you comport yourself as Mother and I have raised you: like a lady!"

I didn't respond to his onslaught. I knew in my heart I had done nothing wrong. But I also knew that I had dreadfully upset and disappointed my father whom I loved and respected. From that day on, I knew that I did not want to live in a country where I couldn't even share a laugh with a stranger.

Sweden's political atmosphere also made me uneasy. Though I wasn't particularly active in that area, I felt there was something wrong with the socialist idea of equality. If someone happened to be smart, worked hard, and made more money than the next guy, I felt that person should be allowed to keep most of it, and not be taxed to the point where the incentive to work was lost. The thought of living in another country returned to me time and again.

I soon realized that, if I really wanted to learn to speak English, *proper* English, I would have to go to England. The various English courses I took at the University of Stockholm were not enough for me to become completely fluent and to travel the world, as I wanted. So, when Aunt Elsa called and said that some friends of hers needed a servant in a huge 16th century castle outside of Bath, in England, I jumped at the chance. The fact that I would be a maid didn't concern me; I would be living in a castle! However, it greatly concerned my parents, though not for the reasons I imagined. My father was not so much concerned about my servitude, but more about whether I would know how to *behave* like a servant.

"Remember," he said, "that when you serve at the table, you mustn't listen to what the people are saying to each other. You must pretend that you don't hear or understand anything. Above all, don't interrupt or laugh as you often do when you help our maid at home."

I promised him I wouldn't.

Sadly, my castle living was not to be. Shortly before my departure, I received a letter that the count had died and, with all the turmoil, they couldn't receive and train a foreign young woman. In my disappointment I flunked my next test, the first time that had ever happened.

However, I was still determined to go to England. One day I saw an ad which read: "Mother's helper wanted, to take care of three children in London; small salary, will be treated as a member of the family." I excitedly applied for the job and was hired. The University would have to wait.

◆   ◆   ◆

So, in 1946 I took the boat from Gothenburg to Tilbury Docks outside London. The trip took a day and a night. I had never traveled on an ocean liner before; in fact, I had never seen an ocean, where sky and water meet, as my only exposure was to the Baltic and the North Sea, where archipelagos obscure the horizon. The voyage was a wonderful experience, only slightly marred by my being seasick.

When I first saw the horizon, I was in awe. I remember Aunt Elsa telling me that, when you see something wonderful and totally awesome for the first time, you should take a picture of it with your mind, so that later you can look at it again and never forget it. That's what I did with my first horizon.

4

Mother's Helper

From Tilbury Docks I took a train to St. Pancras Station, where Mr. David Peirson, my new employer, would meet me at eight o'clock. I had sent him a picture, so he would recognize me. Much to my dismay, at eight o'clock nobody was there.

I waited, and waited some more and after about an hour I tried to call him. In a red telephone booth I found his number and tried to figure out how to dial. After a few false starts, I heard a voice, which said, "Norah Peirson speaking."

"Hello," I replied, "I'm Kerstin, and I am at St. Pancras Station."

"Hello," she repeated again and again.

We continued this ridiculous conversation, until I hung up in frustration. It was obvious that she couldn't hear me. What to do? Not far from the telephone booth stood a man in uniform, wearing a big helmet, whom I recognized as a London *bobby,* because we had read about them in school. I went up to him and informed him that there was something wrong with the phone: I could hear the person on the other end, but she obviously couldn't hear me.

"Did you press button 'A,' young lady?"

"Button 'A'?"

"Yes. When the person you want to talk to answers, you must press button 'A'; otherwise she cannot hear you."

So I tried again, this time pressing the A button and told Mrs. Peirson, that I had arrived and had already been waiting over an hour.

"But you were not supposed to come until eight o'clock," said Mrs. Peirson, very surprised.

"Well, it's nine thirty now," I answered.

"But we thought eight o'clock in the evening," she said.

"We call that twenty o'clock in Sweden," I answered, trying not to sound impatient, and then waited another hour until Mr. Peirson came to pick me up.

The ride from the station to the Peirson's house was several hours long, during which time I had my first experiences of the horrors war could inflict. Coming from neutral Sweden I was totally unprepared for it; enormous buildings reduced to mountains of rubble, streets with gaping holes in them, ragged and dirty children begging in the streets, and amputees, pitifully trying to move in improvised wheelchairs.

When we arrived to the Peirson's home in Finchley, near Hampstead Heath, I saw to my relief, that their home and the neighborhood had escaped the bombings. By this time I was emotionally drained and was wondering if I had made the right decision to come to London so close after the war. That night, the first of many, I cried myself to sleep. I felt very lonely.

The children I took care of were John, age seven, Margaret, age five, and Ruth, who was only two years old. They seemed intelligent, but were not very friendly and were definitely not well behaved. As the youngest of four, I had no experience whatsoever with little children, so was overwhelmed by the responsibility. The fact that both of their parents had degrees in child psychology didn't help me feel less intimidated by the responsibility either.

One day John spat in my face. I became very angry, shook him hard and told him that, if he ever did that again, I would really punish him. He ran to his mother crying. She became furious with me and told me about all the future problems John might have as a result of what I had done. I was very distressed by this. "So what should I have done? Spit back?" I asked. She didn't answer.

My duties included dressing the children, cooking their meals, feeding them, and taking them for walks, playing with them and putting them to bed. I also learned how to iron clothes and to polish silver, knowledge that has served me well for the rest of my life. The only other help in the house was a cleaning lady, who came once a week. Cooking for the children was not easy; first, because I didn't know how to cook and second, because everything was rationed or in powdered form. In order to make an omelet, one had to mix powdered eggs with powdered milk and fry it in the amount of fat you get out of a piece of bacon the size of a postage stamp. Though I felt I should give my ration cards to the Peirsons, I sold them on the black market in order to add to my meager salary.

The children's parents were out every night of the week except Tuesday, my day off, because they wanted to make up for all the miserable nights they had spent in bomb shelters during the war. Every time a plane flew over, John automatically headed for the bomb shelter in the garden.

Despite our occasional disagreements on child rearing, the Peirsons treated me well; I ate my dinner with them, and I was always introduced to their friends. I was also grateful for the aspects of European culture, which they showed to me. Mrs. Peirson gave me books to read in order to help me improve my English, one of which was William Thackeray's *Vanity Fair*, which I thought was very boring. Mr. Peirson patiently took me to many of the museums in London. In one instance, after viewing Delacroix's *The Rape of the Sabine Women* for the first time, I asked Mr. Peirson what "rape" meant. He blushed and suggested, "Why don't you look it up in your dictionary?"

◆   ◆   ◆

One day the phone rang, and Mrs. Peirson said it was for me. I couldn't imagine who it could be since I didn't know anybody in London. When I answered, I heard a man's voice explaining to me that he was John Stuart-Brown, a friend of Aunt Elsa's, and that she had asked him to call me. I accepted his invitation to go with him to a nightclub, very excited at the prospect, as I'd never been to one before. I put on my best outfit for our night out, a red wool dress with a lace collar. My mother had made it and she once told me, it was the prettiest dress she had ever made.

When Mr. Stuart-Brown came to pick me up, I felt very elegant wearing it, until I saw the other woman in the car: a gorgeous woman in a tight black silk dress, embroidered with pearls. Mr. Stuart-Jones introduced her as his fiancée, Olive.

Olive? The only olive I had ever heard of was a little green or black vegetable. How could her name be Olive? She might as well have been called *cucumber* or *carrot*!

After Mr. Stuart-Jones had the unique experience of entering one of London's most exclusive nightclubs with his elegant fiancée and a frumpy teenager from Sweden in a homemade dress, he never asked me out again.

I had no friends in London and was quite lonely so, when my Swedish boyfriend Erik wrote that he had enrolled in a foreign student program at London University, I was deliriously happy. However, I felt he took an eternity to get in touch again and I continued crying myself to sleep.

When he finally called, we arranged to meet at Hampstead Heath, which was halfway between the university and where I lived. I washed my hair and wrapped it in curlers, painted my nails, and spent hours deciding what to wear (not that there was much to choose from in my meager wardrobe). I decided to bike to our meeting place, which I did faster than I ever had in my whole life.

We met at the entrance of the Heath, and I rushed into his arms to kiss him, but could immediately sense that this was not the same Erik whom I had left four months ago in Sweden. He seemed cold and embarrassed. When I asked what was the matter, he wasted no time in telling me that he had fallen in love with an Indian girl whom he had met at the University. He ended the conversation with, "goodbye, I hope that we can still be friends," then biked away.

I returned the same way I had come, but much more slowly this time. The Piersons must have noticed my unhappiness; I think that's why they told me about the Cosmopolitan Club where students from all over Europe gathered to listen to lectures about the English language and to get to know each other. On my day off, that's where I went from then on.

Many of the students at the Club were French. On one occasion, when we examined the differences between speaking French and English, the professor explained, "When we speak English, we speak almost without moving our lips, with our mouths almost closed, maybe so as not to let the fog in. The French, on the other hand, speak moving their lips a lot, so as to keep them always supple, presumably ready for the kissing position."

To practice our English we had to tell the class, what we had been doing since we last met. One French girl, Marguerite, told she had discovered, that the coin-operated heater she had in her apartment, worked just as well with French francs as with English shillings. Since, at the time, there were fifty francs to the shilling, I decided she was a girl, whom I'd like to know better. So I befriended her and we are friends to this day. I also met a very charming Englishman, Bernard Somerset, whom I liked a lot, and dated a couple of times. He was older than I, much more mature and well educated. He taught me so much about English history, litera- ture and customs. I was fond of him, but I was not in love with him. I still was in love with Erik.

One day a girl from Czechoslovakia, *Jarka*, who was part of our gang, said she needed some advice. She had just received information from a friend at the Czechoslovakian embassy that, if she wanted to return to her country within a foreseeable future, she had better return immediately, because a Communist take-over was imminent.

"What do you think I should do?" she asked us. "If I go back, I may never be able to get out of the country, just like in the Soviet Union. On the other hand, if I don't go, I may never see my parents and my boyfriend again."

Most of Jarka's friends advised her not to go. They told her, "You will be mis- erable under the Communist regime and will probably be given a stiff penalty for having lived in a foreign capitalist country. Also, you will never again be allowed to travel abroad."

I was one of the few, who advised her to go. "How can you *not* go, and risk never seeing your parents and boyfriend again? You'll regret it for the rest of your life! I could never do that!" That was easy for me to say, with family and friends in safe Sweden and with no experiences at all of wars, revolutions and political strife.

Jarka took my advice, an advice I have always regretted. None of us ever heard from her again.

◆   ◆   ◆

Shortly afterwards I returned to Sweden. I was happy to be back and I certainly didn't miss those bratty Peirson children. However, there was to my great surprise a letter waiting for me from Bernard. The letter was beautiful, telling me how much he loved me and missed me. It started with, "Dearest Darling," and ended with, "Love and kisses." When I wrote him back, it was very important to me, that my phrasing was correct so I figured that, if I copied his greetings, salutations and loving phrases, I couldn't go wrong.

After we had corresponded for a couple of months, he asked if he could come to see me in Sweden. He said that he would like to meet my parents, a request that surprised me, and which I was not particularly interested in. Erik had returned, and since he had broken up with his Indian girlfriend, we were dating again. All the same, I wrote Bernard that he could visit, and that my parents would be happy to welcome him. My mother loved having the opportunity to practice her English.

Little did I know that the reason he wanted to see my parents, especially my father, was to ask for my hand in marriage! I was not yet twenty-one, and had three more years left at the university. Then I had to work to pay off my student loan. Marriage was the farthest from my mind. I also wanted to travel; see the world.

Bernard was devastated by the news when he arrived.

"But you wrote such wonderful love letters," he said. "You said you missed me and couldn't wait to see me again!"

And then he broke down and cried. That was the first time I had ever seen a grown man cry, and I felt terribly guilty. I realized then, that he had taken my copies of his loving phrases as expressions of my genuine feelings.

5

France

The year with the Peirsons and the correspondence with Bernard gave me a good grasp of the English language and I had no difficulties at all passing the English exam. I was now ready to study French, which was a great deal more difficult. I worked hard at it though, and after I had passed my first exam, I felt that I had earned a break.

When I saw a notice on the bulletin board at the University, "Extras wanted for movie; no experience necessary; twenty *kronor* a day," I decided this was for me. Here was my chance to get into the movies, and maybe become a star. Besides, twenty *kronor* a day was a lot of money for a poor student. Add to that the pleasure of meeting and mingling with movie stars! I immediately applied with about four hundred others. I was picked and told to be at the studio at seven o'clock the following Monday morning.

The movie was *Singoalla*, after a medieval Swedish epic by the Nobel price winner, Viktor Rydberg. Alf Kjellin and Viveka Lindfors, who were stars in Sweden at the time and later on well-known in Hollywood, played the lead roles. My part was to be a victim of the Plague, which meant I was made up with blisters and bumps all over my face—no chance of being recognized by my friends! Even my mother would not have recognized me. The movie was shot in collaboration with a French movie company, and many of the people who worked on it were French. Among them was the costume designer, Marcel Escoffier, grandson of the famous chef Escoffier.

When the directors found out that I could speak French, they said that my talents were wasted as an extra, and they hired me as an interpreter. I interpreted between Marcel and the Swedish seamstresses, an opportunity, which was very exciting and improved my French tremendously.

Marcel and I became good friends and, since I planned to go to Paris to study during the summer vacation, I asked him if he knew of an inexpensive hotel or boarding house near the Sorbonne University.

"But you can come and stay with me. I live near the Sorbonne," he said.

I was shocked. What kind of a girl did he think I was? How could I live with a single man? And in Paris! What would my parents say? For a young girl in the 1940's, brought up in a small town by conservative parents, this was inconceivable.

I stammered a "no, thank you," and left quickly. Later I told one of the seamstresses of the shocking proposition Marcel had made. First she looked puzzled and then she burst out laughing.

"You mean you don't know? You'd be as safe with him as with your own brother! He is gay, for heaven's sake!"

"Gay?" I asked, puzzled.

"Yes, gay, homosexual. He likes boys."

That was how I first heard about homosexuality, but I still didn't take Marcel up on his offer.

(Many years later when my daughter was about fourteen, I decided I didn't want her to grow up as ignorant as I had been, so I told her about gay men. She listened carefully, without interrupting. When I finished, she asked," Mama, now would you like me to tell you about lesbians?")

◆   ◆   ◆

In spite of what I learned at the university and especially from working on the French movie, I felt I should live in France to learn more. Though my first thought was to study at the Sorbonne, it proved to be too expensive. My experience with the Pierson family in London had taught me that speaking with children is a great way to learn a language. Grown-ups will make an effort to understand, while children won't; they just think you are weird. Also, if they don't understand, of course they don't obey. If you tell them as I did, *marcher* (to walk) when you mean *manger* (to eat) you never get the desired result. That's a great motivation to learn how to speak a foreign language correctly. So, during the summer break, I accepted a job as a nanny in France.

My French friend from my London days, Marguerite, found me a position with Dr. and Madame Dauvergne, who had three children. They lived in a little town called Oyonnax, not far from Lyon. During my first evening with the family, Madame Dauvergne asked me, *"Christine, avez-vous des frères et des sours?"* (Do you have any brothers and sisters?) I was in shock. Here was a real French person, who spoke to me in French and who didn't understand either English or

Swedish. I had to answer in French! I stuttered. I stammered. It was awful and terribly embarrassing.

It didn't help when they served what I thought was a cake. I took a normal-sized piece; however, it turned out to be a wheel of Brie cheese, and everybody else took about a tenth of what I had taken. The cheese tasted awful to my Swedish palate.

The cultural misunderstandings continued. When Madame Dauvergne took me for a visit to the Mayor's house for tea, his wife passed the sugar bowl to me, asking, "*Du sucre?*" and before I had a chance to answer, Madame Dauvergne said, "*Pas de sucre*. (No, you don't take sugar,") and took the bowl away. Since I *wanted* sugar in my tea, I was annoyed, until I realized, that sugar was still rationed three years after the war.

When I needed sanitary napkins, I didn't know what to call them in French. So I tried to look it up in my Swedish-French dictionary, but couldn't find it. Then I remembered that we had been using homemade washable napkins in Sweden and, what we called them, I couldn't remember. So, I looked up *sanitary napkin* in the English-French dictionary, and there I found it, *serviette periodique*. They were different somehow, but I put one on. Everything was fine. That is, until I took it off to change. Oh, that hurt! I had put the soft side against my panties and the sticky side against my skin!

Once when I was constipated, I asked Dr. Dauvergne for help. He gave me a pill, the biggest pill I had ever seen. It was huge! I wondered how in the world I would be able to swallow it. Just as I was about to put it in my mouth, Dr. Dauvergne called out in horror,"Non, Non, Non, Christine, you don't put it in your *mouth*; you put it *there,"*and he pointed at my rear end.

That's how I learned about *suppositories!*

The Dauvergne children, François, age six, Nanette, age four and Catherine, only fifteen months old, were much easier to take care of than my English charges. They were well behaved, obedient and charming. The best time I had with them was the month in their summerhouse in Evian on the French side of Lake Geneva.

One day in my free time I rented a *pedalo*, a type of water cycle, and started to make my way to the Swiss town, *Montreux*, on the other side of the lake, inspired by Aunt Elsa's tales of the place. After a couple of hours of strenuous pedaling I only covered one twentieth of the distance. Once again, I took off on the spur of the moment without any planning. Totally exhausted, I had to turn back.

An Innocent Abroad

After four months with the Dauvergnes, my French improved and I could understand most of what was said to me. I planned to spend the rest of my vacation in Paris with my new Swedish boyfriend, Peder, who worked at the Swedish Embassy, spoke French fluently and knew Paris well. We agreed to meet at the Embassy but, when I arrived there, I only found a letter, telling me that he had been delayed in Sweden and to "hang on; I'll be there in ten days." That was easy for him to say, but I had very little money and nowhere to stay.

Luckily I found a room to share at *Union Chrétienne de Jeunes Filles* (YWCA) and had just enough money to pay for a week, but nothing to spend on food. After living on baguettes and water for two days, I knew I had to get a job. But what was I qualified to do?

In the luxury stores on the Champs Elysées I had seen signs, "English spoken," "*Man spricht Deutsch,*" "*Se habla Español,*" so I went into one of them and asked, "Would you like to be able to add *Man talar svenska?*" (Swedish spoken). Though it seemed to me a perfectly reasonable question, they just looked at me astonished and answered, "*Pourquoi?*" (Why?) So I bought a paper and looked at the want ads. I was lucky; I found an ad: "Scandinavian hostess wanted at *Club de Bridge Scandinave*, in the Trocadéro district, to be hat check girl, set up bridge tables, serve tea and perform various other duties; some salary, room and three meals a day."

Three meals a day! I was sold. I took the subway, since it was too far to walk. I certainly had no money for a taxi. The Trocadéro was a nice district, and the club looked respectable. I rang the bell and a woman opened. She was a woman, who must have been pretty once but had aged badly; there was coarseness about her, and she smelled of cheap perfume.

"Bonjour, Madame," I said, "I am here about the hostess position you advertised. I am Swedish and understand Norwegian and Danish,"

She looked me over critically and said, "*Bon.* I'll try you out. I want you to move in and start right away."

While I was talking with her, I could smell something delicious coming from the kitchen. By this time I was salivating and my stomach was grumbling.

"Yes, I can start right away but I can't move in until the end of the month, because my roommate depends on me until then."

"I'd much prefer that you move in right away. But if you can't, then *I insist* that you move in at the end of the month. You won't get paid until you move in."

I said nothing. I wasn't about to tell her that I was planning to work for only ten days!

And so I started. The guests were all men, mostly Swedes and Norwegians. I took their hats and coats, set up bridge tables and served them tea or whatever they wanted. That part was pleasant enough, but I had other duties as well. I had to vacuum and dust, scrub floors, and clean bathrooms. But I didn't mind. The three meals a day more than made up for it. Sometimes I had to serve breakfast upstairs, where there were rooms as in a hotel. Frequently the guests wanted breakfast in bed. After awhile I noticed that, whereas the gentlemen were different each morning, the ladies seemed to be the same. But I didn't pay much attention to them. After their breakfast, it was my turn. Café au lait, croissants and marmalade. Yummy!

The ten days went by fast, and my boyfriend arrived. I told Madame, that I had an emergency in Sweden and had to leave immediately. She was furious, but what could she do?

The next day the newspapers all over Paris reported that the police had raided a brothel in le Trocadéro, *Club de Bridge Scandinave*, my former workplace. The papers reported the names of all the employees, but not mine. I'd fortunately quit the day before, clueless about the goings-on at the club.

After a wonderful week in Paris with my boyfriend I returned to Stockholm, where nobody knew or would *ever* know, that I had worked in a brothel.

I started studying Spanish and, since my French definitely had improved by my living in France, I decided my Spanish would, too. Once again, inspired by Aunt Elsa's journeys and knowing, that what Spanish I had learnt at the university, wasn't enough, I went to Spain.

6

Spain

I received thirty-two responses to my ad in the Spanish newspaper, which read: "Swedish girl looking for Spanish family to live with. Will teach English and French conversation in exchange for room and board."

Thirty were from young Spanish men, who were glad to have me live with them in exchange for room and board, but I had a feeling they were not particularly interested in either French or English conversation. Then there was one from the Mother Superior of a convent, warning me about the type of answers I might receive to a naive ad like mine.

But one reply was from Señor and Señora *Carreño y Cidoncha*, who wanted me to teach their children English conversation. I accepted the position.

My friend Juan, who had translated the ad into Spanish, couldn't understand why I wanted to go to Spain.

"I escaped from there and won't go back until Franco is dead," he explained.

◆   ◆   ◆

In 1949, Franco ruled Spain with an iron fist. Juan's father was among the opposition leaders, and had been exiled with his wife and children, including Juan. Juan hated Franco with a passion.

I had very little knowledge or interest in foreign politics and knew next to nothing about Spain. But to learn to speak Spanish, I knew that I had to go there. In those days, hardly any foreigners went to Spain. The country was still suffering from the Civil War, and Franco discouraged foreign visitors by the foreign currency exchange rate, so that visitors got very few pesetas for dollars, pounds, or Swedish *kronor*. That didn't bother me, because I had very few *kronor* to exchange.

My father was not happy about my decision. Nobody he knew had ever been to Franco's Spain, and he was worried about his youngest daughter, only twenty-two years old. He contacted the Swedish Embassy in Madrid to get some information about "those Carreños." The embassy representative reported back that my host family was honest, with a good reputation but with modest means. I would have to share a room with their daughter Angelita, and the facilities were extremely primitive by Swedish standards. I was surprised to find out that the toilet was a hole in the floor with two platforms for your feet. There were two faucets, one for flushing and the other for the shower. If you made a mistake, well, too bad! I decided I didn't mind; I wanted to learn Spanish.

The Carreños were an attractive family. The father, Antonio, was a good-looking man in his late forties, somewhat portly already and beginning to go bald. His wife, Angela, was about five years younger, a roly-poly, happy woman, who loved nothing better than to cook for her family and anybody else who came along. Their children, Angelita and Antonio Jr., were charming, well-behaved teenagers. They all had black hair and dark eyes, which were particularly appealing and exotic to me.

While all of the Carreños were extremely friendly toward me right from the start, they were also puzzled. They had assumed that I could speak Spanish fluently. My ad had been written perfectly and the letters I sent them before my arrival as well. Of course, Juan had written them. So why was it, that I sometimes didn't understand what they were saying? And why did I rarely talk with them? They spoke so fast and seemed to use totally different words from those I had learned in Spanish class in Stockholm. I pronounced words differently, too, with a different accent. When they asked me, if I was hungry, thirsty or tired, I just nodded and smiled. In fact, nodding and smiling was just about all I did the first week. They also found my behavior strange. While the Spanish would take a siesta after lunch, I would sometimes go for a walk by myself, without a *duena*, or a male escort. No girl from a good family would do such a thing! It became clear to me that they thought I was somewhat retarded, because they had had no contact with foreigners, nor had they been abroad. It was frustrating for me, but also very motivational. The only way I could prove to them, that I *wasn't* retarded, was to learn to speak Spanish. So I learned, and I learned fast. It didn't take long before I understood the meaning of siesta, and what a wonderful custom it is.

The word soon spread that there was a foreigner living with the Carreños and people were curious. I was invited to their homes for dinners and parties. Now I had the opportunity to see how the other half lived. One dinner I attended was given by a Marquesa, who lived in a sixteenth-century castle, where each guest had his own footman standing behind the chair.

The Marquesa invited me to tell about the world outside and what people thought of Spain and of Franco. The guests were also curious about the political and economic situation in Germany and Italy four years after World War II. I could give them very little information in answer to their questions, because I never took much note regarding political issues. Sweden I could tell them about, but somehow that didn't interest them very much!

In the meantime, my Spanish improved. I grew very fond of the Carreños, and they treated me like a member of their family. Every day I taught Antonio and Angelita English, and they made great progress. They were very friendly, showed me respect and introduced me to their friends.

One thing I wanted very much was to have a date with a bullfighter. I asked everybody I knew if they could introduce me to a *torero* or, even better, a *matador*.

One day the phone rang. Señora Carreño answered and said, greatly surprised, "The matador Curro Caro wants to speak with you, Cristina. How does he know *you?*"

I took the phone and a man's deep voice said in Spanish, "I am Curro Caro, and I have been told, that you are Swedish and that you would like to meet me. Well, I would like to meet you, too. Would you like to have lunch with me?"

I was so excited I could barely answer. The Matador Curro Caro wanted to meet *me*! He wanted to have lunch with *me*!

I collected myself and said, "Yes, I would love to."

"Great," he said, "Would you like to meet me tomorrow at one o'clock at Restaurante Valencia?"

"That would be fine," I answered.

"Good," he said and hung up.

When I told Señora Carreño that I was going to have lunch with Curro Caro, she replied, "Well, I am impressed. I would love to meet him!"

The next day I put on my sexiest outfit and took a taxi to the restaurant to meet—The Matador Curro Caro!

As I was looking around I heard a deep voice saying in Spanish, "You must be Cristina, la Sueca." (Swedish woman) "I am Curro Caro."

I turned around. I recognized him immediately from the bullring, even though he wasn't wearing his beautiful *Traje de Luz* (Costume of Light). He was just as handsome in his ordinary clothes, with his dark hair and great body. He had the same sureness in his eyes as he gave me a big smile.

"Yes, I am Cristina," I said, "and I am Swedish. But how do you know about me?"

"Well, a friend told me that you are Swedish and that was enough for me. Swedish girls are very popular here in Spain."

After we had sat down and ordered lunch (Gaspacho and Sangria for me!), he said, "Cristina, have you ever seen a bullfight?"

"Yes, I have. I saw *you* last week! You were magnificent! I witnessed your supreme confidence and control in the ring. Your performance taught me an unforgettable lesson: be intense but unflappable! That could be a lesson for everyone! But tell me, how do you feel when you confront the bull? Aren't you afraid?"

"Oh, no, not at all. The feeling is one of joy, pride and excitement beyond belief, to be the focus of tens of thousands of people who are waiting for he moment of truth."

"The moment of truth?"

"Yes, the moment you kill the bull. But before that, there are so many other moves you must perform: the many different movements with *el capote* (the magenta-colored cape). And then there is my favorite, *El Alarde*, when you turn your back on the bull, or touch his horns.

But enough about me. How about you? Why are you here, and why are there so many Swedish girls coming to Spain?"

"Well, *I* am here to learn Spanish. I don't know why the others are here, but I assume they are searching for s sunshine, beaches and romance, things that are petty scarce in Sweden, especially in the winter."

"So *you* are not looking for romance?"

"Not really. If it happens, it happens."

"When can I see you again? How about tomorrow?"

"Oh, I would love to. But tomorrow I am going to Toledo with the Carreños, and I don't know for how long. But please call me!"

And so ended one of the most fascinating lunches I have ever had! When I returned home, all the Carreños were very curious about my lunch with Curro Caro. I told hem all bout it and added that he would call me again.

He never did.

◆   ◆   ◆

One day, Señor Carreño said he wanted to write to my father and tell him how much they enjoyed having me, so I translated the letter into Swedish. My father, who was retired and had plenty of time, replied to Señor Carreño, and I translated his letter into Spanish. Both men were talkative, and long letters were exchanged almost on a daily basis. Having to translate back and forth was becoming annoying. I didn't have the patience and understanding for the task, so soon tried to figure out a way to end it.

Señor Carreño always ended his letters with an old-fashioned polite phrase, *Pongame a los pies de Su Señora*, which basically means, "Best greetings to your wife," but when translated literally says, "Put me at your wife's feet." One time I translated it literally; that was too weird for my father, and the correspondence dwindled.

Shortly before my return to Sweden, Señor Carreño took me aside and told me that the reason he had answered my ad was not merely to teach his children English. Another reason was that he had written an anti-Franco book, which he had wanted me to translate into English and smuggle out of Spain to be published abroad. Publishing it in Spain was too dangerous. He realized now that my Spanish was far from good enough to do that, and that I was too young and inexperienced to be given such a task.

I was flabbergasted. This was something that I couldn't possibly have imagined! I told him I was sorry that I couldn't help him and that he must be disappointed in me. He said, "Not at all. My family and I are so happy to have met you and to know you, and you will always remain our *hija sueca* (Swedish daughter)."

And so it was. Until his death in 1981 Señor Carreño and I corresponded. In the 1950s, after I had moved to America and become an American citizen, Antonio Jr. asked me to sponsor him, so that he could come to the United States to study. I did and he studied and became a medical doctor. Later he brought his fiancée over. They were married, settled in Corpus Christi, Texas, and had four children. The youngest is named Cristina after me, and I am her godmother. They have all come to visit me several times.

I once asked Antonio, if his father's book had ever been published. He said, "No, but after Franco's death my father's wishes for his country came true, anyway: no more dictatorship, a democratically elected government and freedom of speech."

With Ernesto

◆   ◆   ◆

While living in Madrid with the Carreños, I met my first lover. His name was Ernesto Mendoza. When Ernesto heard that I was Swedish, he was immediately interested. He had heard of the "invasion of the *Sueca* "(Swedish woman), a phenomenon described by Michener in his book *Iberia*:

> *"The first result of the Sueca invasion was cataclysmic. I can't tell you, what a thrill swept over the manhood of Spain, when they discovered that such girls were on our beaches and in our parks, looking for sun and romance. In the old days the proudest boast of a Madrileño used to be, 'I know a bull fighter' or 'I'm having an affair with an actress.' Now it is 'I have a Sueca.' To have a Sueca as your mistress, tall and leggy and blond, is the best thing, that can happen to a man these days."*

I had never met such a wonderful man as Ernesto Mendoza. He was very good-looking, tall with dark wavy hair, glittering brown eyes, a sensuous mouth and very broad shoulders. Warm-hearted and kind, he had an infectious laughter, a deep, sexy voice and an excellent sense of humor. What a contrast to the pale reserved Swedish men whom I had met before!

A week after we met I received a red rose, no card, just a rose. More followed for about two weeks, a red rose every day. My friends were naturally curious; and when I said that I thought they were from a man whom I had met at the Marquesa's party, they asked me his name.

"Ernesto," I said. "I don't quite remember his last name. Mendota, maybe? I believe he is a doctor."

"Oh, that must be the surgeon, Dr. Ernesto Mendoza," said Señora Carreño. "I have heard of him and if he is a friend of the Marquesa's, he must be a gentleman."

We fell in love almost immediately. Our first kiss felt as if electricity had gone all the way from his lips to the bottom of my feet. When he caressed me, his hands made me tingle all over, and when we first made love, no lover could have been gentler, more caring, more giving.

Later on I understood how fortunate I was to have been introduced to the art of lovemaking by such a man. And he gave me so much more. He took me to the famous museum, El Prado, to ancient castles, and told me about the glorious history of Spain. He also read to me from Cervantes and the great Spanish poets. We traveled to all the places he loved: Toledo, Aranjuez, Segovia, Sevilla and Granada.

Once he gave me a book called, *España Gloriosa*. In it he wrote a dedication: *"Tierras y gentes de Espana te quieren, y esperan impaciamente que tu las conoscas bien, para que las quieras mas y mejor* (the lands and peoples of Spain love you, and are hoping impatiently that you may get to know them well, in order to love them more and better)."

To leave him was difficult, but I had to get back to Sweden to finish my studies and get my college degree. Just before I left, I was invited to a party where I met a lady who had just returned to Madrid from a two-month trip with her son. When she introduced him to me I was in shock! He was the spitting image of my beloved Ernesto.

◆   ◆   ◆

On my way back to Sweden I stopped in France to visit the family in Oyonnax, whose children I had taken care of the year before. It was great to see them again and they seemed pleased to see me. We had a wonderful time together, only marred by the fact that I missed my period. That had never happened before, so I decided to go to Paris to see my friend Marguerite and ask her advice. She said I was probably pregnant and advised me to get an abortion.

"An abortion?" I cried out. "Isn't that dangerous, and isn't it illegal?"

"Yes," she said, "but I know somebody, who has done it to some friends of mine with good results and who isn't too expensive."

"But I hardly have any money at all," I cried, tears rolling down my cheeks.

"I'll lend you the money and you pay me back, when you can."

The option of keeping the baby never occurred to me. No way could I return to my parents, pregnant by a much older, married Spanish man. They would have been mortified.

Marguerite gave me the address and the next morning I set out to find the abortionist. He lived on the fourth floor in an old apartment house with no elevator. Walking up those stairs was one of the most painful things I have ever done. I stumbled and almost fell, when a big rat ran by me. When I came to his door, his name was scribbled on a dirty little piece of paper tacked to the front. I found the doorbell, put my finger on it and—I couldn't do it! I couldn't press the button. The thought that a man I didn't know would poke into my body was so revolting, that I almost vomited. With tears streaming down my face, I ran down the stairs and all the way to Marguerite's house where I collapsed in her arms. Two days later I had my period.

◆   ◆   ◆

I didn't contact Ernesto again until forty years later, well after my divorce. He wrote back and asked me to come to Spain to see him on my next trip to Europe. I agreed, and soon I was sitting on the plane to Madrid, thinking about the glorious times we had had together, and looking at his photograph.

We had agreed to meet at our special place in the park, El Retiro, on the third bench to the left of the lake. How many times had we met there, that summer so long ago, twenty, thirty, or more?

I arrived a little early and looked around remembering his voice, his laughter, and his touch. Children were playing with sailboats, young lovers were walking and holding hands, and an old man plodded slowly along.

Ernesto was late. Wait a minute! That old man, there was something vaguely familiar about him. Could it be? No, impossible! This man wasn't tall, he was bent over. His hair was not black, it was white. The sensuous mouth that I remembered had changed into a straight line. I could not see his eyes behind his thick lenses. His arms hung limp at his sides. He looked at me and said slowly, "Cristina?"

I couldn't bear it.

"No, Señor, my name is Maria."

7

To America

Traveling from Sweden to other European countries had been relatively easy on my pocketbook; trains were not expensive, and you could get a job with a family. However, going to America was different. Au pairs were not common there in the fifties and there were certainly no jobs available for a Swede teaching English. Besides, the trip across was very expensive, whether you went by ship or by plane. All the same, I wanted to go to America. I wanted to see what it was all about, this large country, where people from all over the world had settled and where most of the movies, that I had seen, were filmed, the ones with Tyrone Power and Errol Flynn.

In my young Swedish imagination, America was a country, where almost everybody was rich or could become rich. It was a land of endless opportunities, and I thought that I might have a career in television there. In 1950, I was a part-time radio announcer at Radio Sweden. I read the news on short wave in English, French and Spanish. Television had not yet come to Sweden, but I knew it would before long and I wanted to be ready to work in this new medium. I couldn't learn how to do that in Sweden, but I could in America.

I had just graduated with a *Fil. Kand.* (the equivalent of a B.A.) from the University of Stockholm, and hoped to get a scholarship at an American university. I applied to twenty different universities, including Harvard, Yale, and Princeton, but I wasn't accepted by any of them (I didn't know, that they didn't accept women at that time).

Then I read about a small college in Illinois, Augustana College in Rock Island, which offered a one-year full scholarship to any Swede, who would be willing to teach Swedish for a year. I accepted.

When I told my parents that I was going to America for a year they were shocked. My mother was particularly distraught. "To America? For a year?" she exclaimed, "but we'll never see you again! Nobody comes back from America!"

Hundreds of thousands of Swedes had immigrated to America during the 1800's and very few had come back.

"Of course I'll come back," I said. "The fellowship is only for a year."

"You'll probably marry a rich American and stay," cried my mother.

"Get married? Of course not. I promise I'll come back, when my teaching is finished. Maybe I'll go to California, but then I'll be back. After all, I only have a year's leave from my job at Radio Sweden."

My parents were very skeptical, and mother cried.

"Well," said my father, "I'm proud of you for getting the teaching job, and I can see your mind is made up. Deport yourself in such a way so that the Hård af Segerstad family and Sweden will be proud of you." Then he shook my hand. Mother hugged me and kissed me and cried and made me promise to write at least once a week, a promise I'm afraid I didn't keep.

◆   ◆   ◆

There were not many passenger planes in the fifties, which flew from Sweden to America, and those that did, were expensive. So I decided to go by ship. The Swedish-American Line had two ships: the Gripsholm and the Stockholm. I took the Gripsholm, which left from Gothenburg. Nobody saw me off. I had already said my goodbyes to my parents at the train station in Eskilstuna; so, among all the cheering and waving people on the quay, there was nobody I knew. I felt sad, lonely, and embarrassed, so I started waving, too. Crossing the Atlantic took ten days.

The least expensive ticket on the ship was called steerage. I didn't know what it meant; but, since it was the cheapest, I bought it. Steerage consisted of a long hall in the very bottom of the ship, divided in the middle by a large sheet. Men slept on one side and women on the other in cots, which turned out to be comfortable enough, and there were separate bathrooms. As far as I know, there wasn't a lot of hanky-panky going on, but maybe I slept too soundly.

I felt quite lonely on board; most of the other passengers were couples with children and there was hardly anybody my age to talk to. I was a little uneasy about going so far away to a country, where I didn't know anybody and where there was nobody to meet me, when I arrived.

I had mixed feelings, when we finally docked in New York. The Statue of Liberty was an awesome sight and I thought of all the millions of poor immigrants arriving during the last two hundred years, who probably had felt the way I did.

I was the last passenger off the ship. On board I felt safe, as if I were still on Swedish ground. I watched the trunk with all of my worldly belongings go down the chute and being grabbed by Italian dockworkers. For all I knew, they were all Mafiosi, and I would probably never see my trunk again!

Finally the Swedish captain approached me and said,

"Sorry, young lady, but I'm afraid you have to leave the ship. I can't leave the ship until you do, and my wife is waiting for me. Welcome to America."

"But nobody is waiting for *me*," I burst out, "and I don't know anybody in New York!"

"Well, that's too bad," he replied, "you might have thought of that before you boarded." And with that he showed me the way to the gangplank.

The walk down to the quay was one of the loneliest, most frightening walks of my life. But things didn't turn out so bad, after all. I found my trunk, and a nice man found a taxi for me. I gave the driver the address to a foreign student dormitory at Columbia University, which had been recommended by Augustana College. There I shared a room with a German student, and we talked long into the night. Her presence and the thrill we shared about finally being in America took care of my loneliness.

The next day I boarded a Greyhound bus for Rock Island, Illinois.

The Greyhound bus system in the fifties was quite different from what it is now. The seats were comfortable and reclined, so that they could be slept in. The bus stopped every four hours, so you could get off, go to the restroom, stretch your legs and get something to eat. The journey from N.Y.C. to Rock Island took three days.

In Chicago we stopped for a couple of hours. I decided to get something to eat. As I went by a large store, I saw something absolutely incredible in the window. A dish with at least *five* different kinds of ice cream! In Sweden at that time we only had three kinds. The dish was surrounded by four banana-halves and topped by whipped cream, cherries and nuts. I had to have one and, although it was almost more than I could eat, I managed to consume my first double banana split in its entirety.

Another first occurred, when I got into the store. It was extremely cold in there. Outside it was very hot, so how could it be so cold inside? When I walked out into the street and went in again, the same thing occurred; it was hot outside and cool inside. I could not understand it. I must have gone in and out of the store at least three times to experience the miracle of air conditioning!

The Graduate

Back on the bus I sat next to a nice-looking man, who was traveling with his young daughter. He told me much about America and asked questions about Sweden. I enjoyed the conversation very much. On the second day he asked, if I would mind staying with him and his daughter at a hotel in the next town. He said he had a business meeting that night and didn't want to leave his little girl alone. If I would stay with her, he would pay for dinner, the room, and breakfast the next morning. He would also arrange for me to take the next Greyhound to Rock Island.

I accepted with pleasure, and enjoyed myself at what seemed to me like a luxury hotel. The little girl was no trouble at all. The next day they accompanied me to the Greyhound bus, which took me the rest of the way to Augustana College.

◆　　　◆　　　◆

Augustana is a Lutheran College attended by many students of Swedish descent, best known in the United States for its choir, which tours not only the U.S. but Europe as well. When I got off the bus, the head of the Swedish department, an old white-haired man, greeted me warmly in perfect, but accented, Swedish. His name was Dr. Anderson.

Right away he asked me, whether I wanted to live in a teacher's apartment, or in a dormitory with the students. Having read and seen movies about American dormitories, sororities and fraternities, I thought, that it would be more fun to live with the students than with the old teachers, especially if they were Mr. Anderson's age. So I got a room in a dormitory, which I shared with a teenaged girl of Swedish descent named Karin, who was delighted to share a room with a *real* Swede. All four of her grandparents had emigrated from Sweden.

I taught Swedish two hours a day, and spent the rest of the day studying the subjects required for a BA degree. I took two courses that I thought would be helpful in my future TV carrier in Sweden, Speech and Debate. Those were subjects which at that time were taught nowhere in Sweden. My first subject for debate, "Should the Federal Government adopt a permanent plan for prize-wage control?" was meaningless to me, so my teacher suggested that I read Time Magazine to brush up on current events. In one of my speech classes, we were taught to write commercials for radio and TV. I was skeptical because there were no commercials on state-run Radio Sweden, but I attended the class all the same. One of my attempts ran: "He likes her, she likes him, and they both like Hershey."

At the age of twenty-five I graduated with a BA degree, with the cap and gown and the whole ceremony, which was quite exotic to me. In Sweden you get your diploma in the mail, and that's that. I had learned a lot about America, and my BA degree turned out to be very useful for my subsequent teaching career in the United States, but my social life was boring. Here I was a, "woman of the world," who had lived in many different countries, dated many foreign men, and had had a Spanish lover, now leading the life of a college co-ed in a small Midwestern town. The big thrill of the week was to be taken to the corner drugstore for a malted milk by some boy at least five years my junior! Booooring!

But, that was before I joined the Foreign Students Club and met Ben Fuller. He was a Canadian and was studying to become a chiropractor at Parker School of Chiropractic in Davenport, near Rock Island. He was about my age and we hit it off immediately. I had never met a Canadian before and that made it even more fun. We had picnics, went swimming and even attended the prom. Around the time I decided to go to California, he went back to Canada, so we said our goodbyes and went in opposite directions.

What most attracted me to California, or *Kalifornien* as we called it, was the Pacific Ocean and the palm trees and Hollywood, which I had dreamt of while studying geography in Sweden. Yet there was also another reason; I had been corresponding for a year with my American boyfriend Jack, who lived in L.A. We had met at the University of Stockholm the year before, when he studied town planning on his GI bill. I couldn't wait to see him.

Before leaving, I first tried to get a job as a disc jockey at a local radio station. They had programs in Swedish, since many older listeners still spoke Swedish. My mother had sent me some Swedish records, which I would play and then comment on in Swedish. The station manager agreed and said, that as soon as I got a sponsor, he would pay me. I never did. I was told that they didn't like my accent or the way I spoke Swedish. My accent? The way I spoke Swedish? My Swedish had been perfectly acceptable for Radio Sweden, and its Swedish listeners. If anybody spoke Swedish with an accent, it was the people in Rock Island! I did manage to make some money giving lectures on "Sweden and the Swedes" to Women's Clubs, sewing circles and international organizations for ten dollars a lecture and a free dinner.

Once the president of the local Rotary called the college and asked if the "Professor from Sweden" could come and give a talk on anything he liked. Their lecturer had cancelled and he obviously thought that "Kerstin" was a man. I went along to give the talk and, stepping up to the podium, I found an audience of about three hundred men! I don't know, who was the most surprised, I or the audience, who obviously had expected *Mr.*Kerstin.

I immediately realized, that my little talk about "Sweden and the Swedes" was not at all appropriate for this audience. I told them so and suggested, that if they would like to ask me questions, I'd do my best to answer. The arrangement worked very well, and I knew the answers to most of their questions.

Until one man asked: "Do farmers in Sweden still work their fields with plows and horses?"

"Well, I'm not a country girl, but I think they mostly use National Harvester."

That broke them up. They roared with laughter, stood up and applauded, and I smiled and left the podium. I had no idea what was so funny. How was I to know, that practically all of them worked for John Deere, National Harvester's main competitor?

After that I didn't give any more lectures, but I still needed money for the trip. So I went to the best restaurant in Rock Island, called "Sweden House," and got a job as a waitress. Since I didn't have a green card, only a student visa, they couldn't legally employ me, but if I wanted to work under the table for tips, they'd agree to my employ.

I took the job and, since everything Swedish was very popular, I got good tips, especially after I started wearing my Swedish national costume, which Aunt Elsa had given me. The customers wanted to know about Sweden, places where their parents came from, Swedish words and customs, and other cultural information. In fact, I got tipped quite a bit more than the other waitresses and, after awhile, that caused some envy. I think they mentioned it to the cook, because suddenly he didn't seem to have my orders ready on time, and he made many mistakes.

However, one waitress was very nice to me. One night, when I missed my bus, she invited me to spend the night in her house. We both had the early morning shift, so it made sense. When I walked into her bedroom, I noticed there was only one double bed, which I didn't think anything of at first; it certainly was wide enough for two. But during the night, after she moved closer and closer, I got up and moved to the sofa. The next morning she said she had thought I had understood; that I wanted what she did, and was very apologetic.

"Thought I had understood?" I did know about homosexual men, but women? I quit the job at the restaurant the next day, because I felt too uncomfortable around her now.

Then one day, looking for another job in the newspaper, I saw an ad that two women were looking for a third to share expenses for their trip to California, and I jumped at the opportunity. We were to share the cost for gas and take turns driving. The ad said they wanted a young woman, not over thirty and since I was twenty-five, they accepted me. When I met them, I was surprised, because they were much older than twenty-five, at least in their fifties, but I thought nothing of it.

There was one problem though, a big one, which I hadn't told them: I didn't know how to drive! I figured, that if I told them later, when we were already on our way and had become friends, they would take it better. So, when they suggested that we each drive in two-hour shifts, I said, "You know, I have my period, which makes me very tired. I'd prefer not to drive until tomorrow." That was ok with them.

The next day I told them, "I hate to tell you, but I don't know how to drive."

"What, you don't know how to drive? You agreed to share the driving and you don't know how! You lied to us!"

"I am very sorry," I said, "I'll gladly pay for *all* the gas, in exchange for letting me go with you, because I want so much to see my boyfriend in LA."

They agreed to the arrangement and, although we didn't talk much during that day, by the time we settled into a motel, we were on friendly terms again.

Of course I felt bad about having lied. But I felt a little better about it, when I realized, why they had insisted on a much younger woman to accompany them. Every evening before dinner they insisted I go with them to a bar. Since I didn't drink much in those days, I really didn't want to, but they insisted, and I soon found out why. They had a much better chance to get to know the guys at the bar with a young woman along. I guess you might say I was the bait!

◆   ◆   ◆

I saw a great deal of America during this trip: the Great Plains of the Middle West, the Rocky Mountains, Bryce Canyon, the deserts of Arizona and New Mexico. I had never seen anything like it. The mountains were so big, the deserts so vast, the plains so never ending! For this young girl from Sweden, it was a fascinating experience. My home country had never seemed so small.

We only had one mishap. In the middle of the Arizona desert, the car, an ancient Nash, just stopped. We didn't know what was wrong. Luckily, there was a small gas station not too far away and we managed to push the car there.

The attendant was an old Indian, the first Indian I had ever seen. He was tall, with long dark hair in a braid down his back. He was brown-skinned (not red!) with a large hooked nose. His eyes were black and piercing.

I had read about Indians, of course. Fennimore Cooper's *The Last Mohican* I had read in Swedish. With my brothers I had often played, *Kovboysar och Indianer*, as we called them. When *we* played, the Indians were the good guys.

The Indian took a look under the hood of the car, and said, "Two parts broken, no good."

"Can you repair it?" I asked.

"Not here. I must tow it to a bigger garage in town."

We said ok, gave him the keys, and he left. Only after a few minutes did we realize, how foolish we had been. We had given him the car! There we stood in the middle of the desert without a car, no food and the only thing to drink was the last Coke from the Indian's Coke machine!

We were hungry; we were thirsty, and how did we know, if he'd ever come back? He had our car; he could sell it, for all we knew. Or, he might take so long, that we would starve to death, or die by sunstroke. All that would remain of us would be three skeletons!

He came back two hours later.

During those two hours I was really homesick for Sweden. I wrote a farewell letter to my mother, which she fortunately never received. We drove to L.A. without incident and I was dropped off at Jack's mother's house, where he lived.

I was very happy to see Jack again, but I could tell immediately that this was not the same Jack, whom I had kissed goodbye a year ago in Sweden.

I soon found out why the change. He had another girl friend. That posed a problem. I was upset of course, but I can't truly say that my heart was broken. But I was broke, and now I couldn't very well stay with Jack and his mother. I had already sold my return ticker back to Sweden to finance my cross-country trip.

So with my last dollar I bought a newspaper to look for a job. And I found it. The Army Language School in Monterey wanted a native Swede to teach Swedish to American soldiers and officers. I couldn't imagine why, but that was not my problem. I applied and got the job. And it was a dream job!

8

A Dream Job

"This week I'll plan a dinner date every night with a guy from a different country," I wrote in my diary in Monterey, California, 1952.

Did I? You bet. It was easy. I could have done it for a month. If I had wanted to be naughty, I could have included breakfast as well.

The students were American soldiers and officers, all male between twenty and sixty years of age—about two thousand of them. We teachers were natives of thirty-two different countries—two hundred of us. About one hundred and eighty were men in the same age bracket as the students. That left twenty women for two thousand, one hundred and eighty men. But the ratio for some of us was even better, because at least half of the women were old—over forty!

I was particularly interested in meeting people from countries where I had never been. Dara, from Albania, told me many things about the differences between Albanians, Serbs and Croats. This later made me understand the Balkan wars much better.

Pedro from Brazil taught me a valuable lesson, two actually. When he showed me a picture of himself and his sisters, I noticed his sisters were black. So I said, "Your father must have been married twice."

"No, why?"

"Well, your sisters are black."

"So?"

"Well, you are white, so you and they must have had different mothers."

"Oh, that! No, we didn't. But now that you mention it, I believe one of my grandmothers was black. I have never really thought about it."

Many years later I went to Sao Paolo to visit Pedro and his wife and children. Pedro took me all around, and he pointed out some beautiful women, soliciting on street corners.

"Don't leave me, Pedro, even though they are beautiful," I said, jokingly.

"Don't worry, Cristina." They are not my type. They are guys in women's clothes."

◆   ◆   ◆

Not only was my social life great, but no teacher could have a better working situation. There were no more than eight students in each class, and they studied only one subject, in my case, Swedish—Swedish eight hours a day, five days a week for six months. In addition to this, I was living in one of the most beautiful towns in California. The ocean, the beaches, the palm trees, all these things that I had dreamed of in Sweden, were there at my fingertips. And in the forest there were *kantareller,* those wonderful mushrooms, growing wild and there for the picking!

One might wonder what the purpose was of teaching these American soldiers and officers all these foreign languages. Why Swedish, for instance? Well, who knows? But we teachers were told to teach them, not only the language, but customs, gestures and behavior as well.

We taught them how to use a knife and fork, how to smoke a cigarette and how to propose a toast, so that once in the country they could "melt in" with the population. I suppose we really were training spies and infiltrators. Again, why Swedish? It was a puzzle, since Sweden wasn't even a member of NATO.

I had two black students in my class. They were bright and learned to speak Swedish well. I even taught them Swedish folk dancing. They looked resplendent in red vests and yellow britches with red tassels around their knees. I often wondered how they "melted in" in Sweden. Most Swedes at that time had never seen a black person, except in the movies. That was not my problem though. I had a great job, a lot of fun, and have never since been in a situation where the ratio of men to women was 2180 to 10!

The Korean War was going on. If a student flunked the course, he was sent to Korea. The students worked hard. Never in my teaching career have I had more motivated students.

Except one, Crispino Severini.

He was of Italian descent, spoke fluent Italian, but didn't know how to read and write it. In order to get out of being sent to Korea, he applied to the Army Language School's Italian department.

He was sent to *my* class. When I wanted to move him to the Italian class, which was located across the hall from mine, I ran into all kinds of obstacles. It couldn't be done without the colonel's permission. The colonel couldn't do it without the army's permission and the army couldn't do it without the Pentagon's permission—a typical snafu. I later learned the meaning of that: <u>S</u>ituation <u>n</u>ormal, <u>a</u>ll <u>f</u>ucked <u>u</u>p. Very apt.

Crispino stayed in my class, studying Swedish, in which he was not the least bit interested. Not surprisingly, he failed all the tests. I had to flunk him. Knowing, that if I did that, he most certainly would be sent to Korea, I tried to have him take the class again, to give him extra lessons, to give him one more chance. It couldn't be done. And sure enough, a few months later he was sent to Korea.

A year later I received a letter from his father, telling me that Crispino had been killed in combat. The father wrote that if I hadn't flunked him, his son would still be alive.

That was a difficult fact to live with. How I wished I hadn't flunked him! Sure, I was just following orders. It was not my fault; I had tried to prevent it, and yet, a father had lost his son because of me. I tried to write him a letter. But what good would that have done? Nothing I wrote could bring his son back.

My guilty feelings continue to plague me.

9

The Russian

Our Wedding Picture

I enjoyed meeting all the different nationalities at the Army Language School, but I had not met a Russian yet, and I wanted to very much. I had never met one and thought them very exotic.

The Russian department was separate from the other departments, so we didn't meet one very often. But one night at the Officers' Club my friend Dara introduced me to a Russian instructor. His name was Georgi Alexandrovitch Shirokow, George for short. He was handsome with blue eyes and brown curly hair, and I thought that his Russian accent was very sexy.

One of our first dates was for breakfast. When George asked what I wanted, I said, "I'll have the same thing as you."

"O.K., I think I'll have tea and a bear claw."

A *bear* claw? I was in shock. How could he order a *bear* claw? But, after all, he was a Russian, and maybe they ate that in Russia? I was relieved when the waitress gave me a pastry, which, yes, did have the shape of a bear claw!

We fell in love almost immediately. Maybe it was a case of "opposites attract." We certainly came from very different backgrounds. He had grown up under Stalin's cruel dictatorship and suffered in prison camps in Germany. I remember him saying, "people are no damned good; I much prefer animals." George trusted nobody.

I, on the other hand, had grown up in neutral Sweden, where I had been totally safe and never experienced war. I was very trustful of people.

He didn't speak Swedish and I didn't speak Russian. We spoke English to each other. But we also had things in common; we were both European immigrants in America, we didn't have American passports, and had to speak in a foreign language to survive here.

We became engaged a few months after we met. Now I had a problem on my hands: how to explain to my Swedish parents, that I was going to marry a Russian!

The Swedes hated and despised the Russians. The reason was, that for hundreds of years, wars raged between Russia and Sweden, and Sweden always lost. Russia had taken one third of Sweden's territory, which now is Finland. Finland became independent only in the eighteen hundreds. The hatred and contempt between the Russians and the Swedes was so strong and had lasted so long, that there are still signs of it in the Swedish language today. If a Swede wants to say, "Are you completely out of your mind?" he says the equivalent of, "Are you completely Russian?" When children don't behave, they are told the Russians will come and take them.

So, with trepidation, I waited for an answer to my letter to my parents about my engagement to George. I received two separate letters. My father's was a long one. It described in great detail the Russian-Swedish relations during the last five hundred years. The gist of it was that they had always been bad and would never improve. My mother's letter was shorter. She wrote: "Has it occurred to you that you probably never will sing Swedish lullabies to your children?" But they both said that if I were absolutely sure and determined to marry George, they would give us their blessing and we could have the wedding at home in Sweden.

We were very happy about that; at least, I was. I think George was a little apprehensive about it all, because we were to be married in a Swedish Lutheran church and in Swedish. So George was obliged to repeat in Swedish, what the minister said. That was much more than, "I do."

The wedding day came. The eleventh century church in my small hometown was completely filled. People even stood in the back. I was amazed. I knew that my parents had many friends, but this many? Then I understood. They had not really come for my sake. They had come to see the Russian. Most of them probably had never seen one. Who knows what they expected to see, but as we walked up the isle, I heard a murmur, "*ryss, ryss, ryss.*" (Russian, Russian)

We approached the altar. Now I would find out if George could say the Swedish words.

We had practiced. We had practiced a lot. I thought he knew it perfectly. Well, he did. Almost. When he came to the part: *Jag tar dig till min äkta maka* (I take you as my wedded wife), he made one tiny mistake. Instead of *äkta*, he said "*extra*". The minister heard it, I know, but he pretended not to. My brother who was an usher, stood very near. He wore his parade uniform of the King's Guards, with his saber at his side. His face was like mask, but his saber rattled.

We had the whole ceremony recorded, and George insisted on playing it every anniversary. His constant comment, "You see, I only promised to take you as my *extra* wife."

As if he had known what he was saying!

10

Our First Child

In 1954, when I was pregnant with our first child, I found to my great surprise that baby boys in the United States are routinely circumcised. That was news to me, since in Sweden circumcision is a religious ceremony that only people of the Jewish and Muslim faiths adhere to. But here in America, the practice was apparently a common one for all boys. The reason I was given was it is more hygienic.

When I asked my husband about it, he became very upset at the very thought of it.

"Absolutely not! No son of mine will ever be circumcised," he said. "Don't you ever even think about it."

"I think you are overreacting," I answered. He then told me about an incident that had happened during World War II in Germany. He had spent most of the war in a prison camp in Aschaffenburg, Germany, imprisoned there after the Germans invaded his hometown Kharkov in Ukraine, in what was then the Soviet Union.

One day all the male prisoners were called out and told to stand at attention. Then they were ordered to drop their trousers. A German soldier inspected their penises. All who were circumcised were shot on the spot.

"So you see," said George, "why I don't want our son circumcised. Anti-Semitism has a long history all over the world, and you never know what might happen to him."

Considering what George had been through, I understood perfectly. But the baby would be *mine* too, and, if a boy, I wanted what was best for him. If there were any advantages to circumcision, any at all, I wanted at least to know about them so as to make an informed decision. The next time I went to my obstetrician for my regular check-up, I asked him to explain to me all the possible advantages and disadvantages of circumcision.

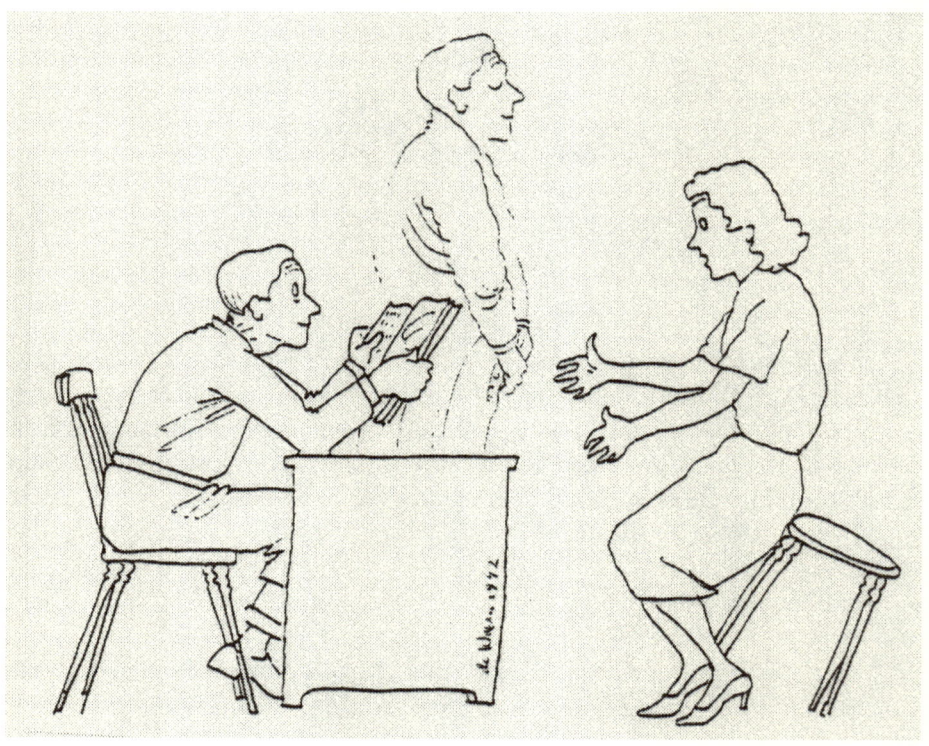

Is He Going To Show Me *His*?

His name was Abe Goldstein. He was a good friend of ours, and I felt he would give an unbiased opinion. When I asked him the question, he said,

"Have you ever seen a circumcised penis?"

"No," I answered.

"Well, then let me show you." Then he walked towards me.

"My God!" I thought. "Is he going to show me *his?*

The shock must have shown on my face, because Abe burst out laughing.

"Oh, no, we're not going to have that much fun," he said. "All I'm going to show you is a picture in a book on the bookcase behind you." He took the book from the shelf and explained the pros and the cons of circumcision. But I was too embarrassed to pay much attention. To this day, I really don't have an opinion one way or the other.

Abe Goldstein thought the incident was hilarious and told everybody what "Kerstin thought I would show her."

The final irony: we had a girl!

Katya's First Christmas

When our daughter Katya was six months old, I thought the time had come to have her baptized. I had no particular religious reason, but baptism was a custom in our family. We were all baptized Lutherans, since that was the state religion in Sweden.

One day I mentioned this to George. I said," As far as I am concerned, we can have her baptized in the Russian Orthodox Church if you prefer, since that is your father's religion. Grandpa adores Katya and I think that would please him very much."

George had no religion, being born and brought up in the Soviet Union, where the Communists considered any religion "the opiate of the people." Not only that, but George was completely *ignorant* of any kind of religion. The Russian Orthodox Church, which had dominated all of Russia before the Communist revolution, didn't exist anymore. The splendid cathedrals and churches were turned into warehouses and, sometimes, prisons.

So George, being a practical man whose main goal was to make money for his family, said, "We must consider what is best for our daughter. We should give Katya a religion that will be useful for her in America. Why don't we baptize her a Rotarian? I have heard a lot of good things about Rotarians, and many of them are quite wealthy."

After I explained to him what Rotary was, he agreed to baptize her a Lutheran; one of the few times he followed my advice! Generally with George, it was either his way or no way.

11

Becoming an American

A couple of years after Katya was born, my husband, after five years in the United States, was eligible for citizenship. We had a little party to celebrate the occasion. I'll always remember how he happy he was when he said, "I finally have a country to be proud of."

With me it was different. I never intended to give up my Swedish citizenship. I was very proud and pleased to be Swedish. Most Swedes feel that way. I believe the smaller the country, the more patriotic the people. So I wasn't at all sure if I wanted to become an American. Most of my European friends completely understood.

My good friend Julia de la Cuadra from Spain was shocked at the very thought of it.

"It's as if the Greeks had voluntarily agreed to become Romans," she said. My Swedish friends and relatives felt even more strongly about it. My father never understood, how I could consider such a thing.

"To be born a Swede, by the grace of God, and then to become, of all things, 'an American'" was how he expressed his dismay. He had never been to the United States, and did not speak a word of English.

Then the CIA hired my husband as a Russian specialist and George, our daughter Katya, my father-in-law and I moved to Washington D.C. for his training. I didn't know what he was being trained for. (After all, it was CIA.)

One day George came home from his school and announced, "We are moving to Japan!"

"To Japan? Where in Japan? When? We don't know anybody there! We don't speak Japanese! What about Katya and grandpa?"

"Calm down. Don't worry; it is all taken care of! We'll leave in three weeks!"

I was in shock, but at the same time delighted. Japan, how exotic! Not even Aunt Elsa had been there!

Since George's work was not entirely without danger, his employers felt that we would be safer if everybody in the family were an American and thus under the protection of the American embassy. So it was strongly suggested I become an American citizen. Dual citizenship did not exist then. And I had to admit that the American Embassy was better equipped to protect me, if need be, than the Swedish. So I agreed. I have never regretted it.

To become an American citizen in 1956 was not easy. First of all, your English had to be perfect: but more than that, you had to be familiar with American history, geography, institutions and the constitution. You had to know how the federal, state and local governments worked, were elected and much, much more. All prospective citizens were given a little green book full of facts pertaining to the above. There was a lot to learn.

The day came for my examination. I had to appear before a court clerk on a Wednesday between three and four. I was to bring with me an American citizen, who had known me for five years and could vouch for my good character. Since I had been in the U.S. only *four* years, which presented a bit of a problem. When I pointed this out to the immigration authorities, I was told that they just followed regulations.

At three o'clock on the appointed day, I appeared with a good friend, who had known me for a couple of years. The clerk, who was to examine me, was a short, skinny guy, almost bald. He had apparently cut himself when shaving, because he had a Band-Aid on one side of his chin and bristles on the other. I generally like men, especially good looking ones. This one though was *not* good looking.

He was just about to leave when we arrived.

"Something has come up," he said. "Please come back tomorrow."

When I objected to his having wasted my time and that of my witness's, he just shrugged his shoulders and said, "This way you will have another day to study your little green book."

I was furious, and sputtered in his face, "I already know that green book from cover to cover!"

This is not the smartest thing to say to the person who is going to examine you.

The next day my friend and I presented ourselves before the clerk, again. When he saw me, he said in a voice dripping with sarcasm: "Oh, yes, I remember you. You are the young lady, who knows the little green book from cover to cover. Well, well, we'll soon see about that."

I knew then what I was in for. However, he could not flunk me. Higher authorities than this little pip-squeak wanted me to become an American citizen;

there was not a thing he could do about it. After all, the CIA had requested it. And he knew that I knew that. But that was not going to prevent him from having some fun with me.

His first question was, "Explain the meaning of *gerrymander*."

I didn't have a clue. (It is a device for re-designing voting districts in such a way so as to increase or decrease the number of a certain type of voter.) I do not remember the rest of the questions, but they were equally obscure. Every once in a while he would stop and ask, "Excuse me, but I am a little confused. Aren't you the young lady who said you *knew* the little green book?"

Oh, he was having so much fun!

Finally he said, "I hope this question isn't too difficult for you. What are the colors of the American flag?"

A few days later in a big hall in the Federal Court House in Washington, I, plus several hundred other future Americans, were given our new citizenships. We swore allegiance to our new country and to its flag (whose colors I knew!) and were told by the judge, "Remember, you are now Americans. Not German-Americans, nor French-Americans nor Swedish-Americans. Just Americans. There is no such thing as a hyphenated American."

12

Our Polyglot Daughter

When we were living in Washington, D.C., I spent much more time with my father-in-law than I did with my husband. George's CIA training was rigorous; he left early in the morning and came home exhausted late at night.

Two years earlier, when our daughter Katya was born in Monterey, California, my Russian father-in-law had come to live with us. He didn't speak a word of English; so, if I wanted to speak with him, I had to learn Russian. George taught me one Russian phrase: "*ya ochen rada shto vui o nas.* (I am very happy to have you here)." Not necessarily true, but what else could I say?

My father-in-law and I often went for walks in the park with two-year-old Katya and watched her in the playground. He told me about life in czarist Russia and during the revolution. Since he spoke only Russian, I began to learn it too, and we spoke Russian to Katya.

One day she fell from the top of a slide in the playground. She was bleeding from a deep gash in her head. I called an ambulance, which drove us to the hospital. As we entered the emergency room, the nurse said, "Be sure to tell your little girl to hold absolutely still. The cut has to be stitched, and she is too young for anesthetics."

"But I don't know how to tell her that in Russian," I answered, almost in panic.

"In Russian? Why Russian? Tell her in English for heaven's sake!"

"But she doesn't understand English. She only speaks Russian."

"In others words, you can't speak to your own daughter?"

I didn't answer and when poor Katya screamed, as the doctor started stitching, I held her tight and sang a Russian lullaby. Luckily my daughter held still and was successfully stitched up. The next day I started speaking to her in English.

Katya and Friends

"Grandpa" became the baby-sitter. He adored his little granddaughter, and spoke to her in Russian, of course, the only language he knew. I learned along with her. My Russian was on the level of a two-year-old's, which was my daughter's age, when the accident happened in Washington, D.C.

I wanted my parents and brothers and sister to see my "half-Russian" daughter and to allow her Swedish grandpa equal time with her Russian one; so, after we had settled in Washington, I took her with me to Sweden. When we arrived in Stockholm, my father was there to meet us. Snow was beginning to fall, which, of course, was something entirely new to my California-born daughter. To my father's great delight she said in Russian, "*Belai dosht*" (white rain). My father was greatly impressed (he had learned Russian in school) and would forever bore his friends at the club about his extremely gifted granddaughter.

After the incident in the hospital I spoke only English with Katya. But, if she wanted to get something from her Russian grandfather, she naturally had to ask for it in Russian. That is an excellent motivation to learn a language.

Not long after the trip to Sweden, we moved to Japan. We lived in Tokyo surrounded by Japanese, who had many children. When they found out there was a little blond, blue-eyed girl living in their midst, they were very curious, and they often came over to our gate and called, "*Katyachan, asomibasho!*" (Katya, come out and play!") She did, and soon she spoke Japanese as well as they did.

Katya became quite a curiosity for the grown-ups. The Japanese love children and often invited her to their homes. Not only did she learn to speak better and better, but she also absorbed their manners and mentality. Her Japanese soon became much better than mine, and I frequently used her as my interpreter. Once, when we were caught in a rainstorm, I asked her to go into a store and borrow an umbrella (that was common practice; you returned it at your convenience). Since it was late, I asked her to hurry. She took her time, and I was quite angry, when she came back.

"Why did you take so long? I told you to hurry!"

"But Mama, you don't understand. You can't just go in and ask for an umbrella! You have to ask how *obasan* (grandpa) is and how *ojisan* (grandma) is and listen to how they are!" said my daughter almost in tears, poor thing—caught between two cultures.

◆   ◆   ◆

Katya has now added Italian (since we lived in Italy for three years) and French (she was an au pair in France) to her other languages. She produces wild life films, which are shown all over the world. Her twelve-year old son goes to Lycée Français and speaks fluent French.

13

Japan

For an American to live in Japan in the late fifties and early sixties was not easy. We were not welcome there. Considering what had happened during the war, that's easy to understand. But it was more than that. We were not merely disliked as the former enemy. To the Japanese we were very unattractive, grotesque almost. We were too big; we had colorless hair and colorless eyes and our noses were huge. We had bad manners and laughed too loudly. We didn't bow to each other; instead we touched each other!

We had a completely different mentality. For instance, it was impolite for a Japanese to say, "no." If you asked a plumber, when he could come to fix a broken pipe, he would ask, "When would you like me to come?"

If you said, "Can you come Monday?" he would always say, "yes." That did not necessarily mean, that he would come Monday, but it would have been impolite for him to say, "no." That made dealings between us very frustrating. It took a while for me to understand all that, and didn't make for a very happy time.

I didn't drive in Japan. There were two reasons for this. All the street names were of course in Japanese characters, which I couldn't read. Also, if there were an accident, it was always the foreigner's fault. So I had to take the train or the subway, which was a nightmare.

The trains were so crowded one could hardly breathe. The railroad had special employees at every station, called *oseea,* which means roughly, "push-on-er," whose only job was to squeeze people into an already crammed train compartment. They were very efficient. They put their knee on your butt and pushed. Forget about getting a seat, even if you were a pregnant woman, as I was. No "gentleman" ever gave a seat to a woman; in fact, the woman was expected to give up hers, if a man asked.

I never did that. I know that you should "do in Rome as the Romans do," but really! There are limits. I just said in Swedish, *"jag förstår inte"* (I don't understand) and stayed in my seat.

So when the train stopped, I pushed myself off the train through immovable Japanese men. One day I fainted right on the platform, and apparently lay there for about five minutes. As I came to, with a bump on my head and a sore arm, the first thing I saw was a man's two legs, as he stepped right over me, as if I were a log or something. He didn't even have the courtesy to walk around me. Nobody tried to help me up. The crowds of passers-by totally ignored me.

I picked myself up, caught my balance, wiped the blood from my arm and took a taxi home, quite shaken by the event. The next morning I told what had happened to one of my few Japanese acquaintances. He was not at all surprised.

"You don't understand. Nobody could possibly help you. Such an action would have placed upon your shoulders such a burden of gratitude, which you, especially you, a woman and a foreigner, would never have been able to pay back. Wouldn't that have been awful for you?"

I remember a couple of times when I had helped various young Japanese delivery boys and never even received a "thank you." That was in the fifties when Japanese housewives rarely cooked. Instead they ordered "take-out" from one of the plentiful neighborhood restaurants. Young men on bicycles delivered these meals. They held the trays with food in one hand and balanced the bicycle with the other. The food was kept in beautiful lacquer bowls, and often up to five trays were stacked, one upon the other. Unfortunately, the young men sometimes lost their balance in traffic, and there were bowls and trays all over the street. Whenever I saw it, I would try to help the young men retrieve their bowls, before they were crushed by on-coming traffic. They never thanked me; in fact, they often seemed downright hostile.

Now I know why.

♦   ♦   ♦

To my Swedish friends and relatives, Japan and the Japanese were exotic. Nobody they knew had ever been there, let alone lived there. They often wrote me letters, asking what it was like to live in such a different country, and how I got along with the Japanese without speaking their language.

Since I had worked for Radio Sweden as a newscaster, it occurred to me that maybe I could do a program in Swedish about Japan and send it on short wave to Sweden.

When I approached the people at NHK (Nippon Hosai Kyokai), the Japanese Radio, they liked the idea and they hired me. They suggested I do a weekly program in Swedish, which was beamed on short wave to Sweden.

Interviewing a Japanese Bride

With the help of an interpreter (whose only foreign language was French), I interviewed various Japanese people about typical Japanese customs like the Tea Ceremony and *Ikebana* (flower arrangement).

Sumo Wrestler

When I wanted to interview a Sumo wrestler about his sport, my interpreter suggested I do it in their locker room. Since the wrestlers would presumably be practically naked, I was a little embarrassed at first, but *they* were not.

The Japanese have a different attitude about nakedness from us westerners. They are not the least bit embarrassed about their bodies and do not in anyway connect nakedness with sex. Anyway, behind their enormous stomachs, there was nothing of interest to see.

The Sumo wrestlers place great reliance on weight and bulk. Some of them weigh close to four hundred pounds. They are huge and very strong, but at the same time surprisingly light on their feet.

The wrestling takes place within a ring twelve feet in diameter. The wrestlers are naked but for a loincloth. Each contest is preceded by certain preliminaries of almost religious significance. At the command of the referee the wrestlers crouch opposite each other with their hands on the ground and watch for an opening. The contests are usually short. It is like a game of catch-as-catch-can. The object is for one wrestler to grab the other and throw him on the floor or to lift him out of the ring. After congratulating the champion I asked," Why did you choose such an unusual profession?"

"I did not choose it, my parents chose it for me. I was an unusually large baby; and, since being a Sumo wrestler is a very honorable profession which goes back over a thousand years, they decided I had a good chance of becoming one. So they immediately started feeding me things that would increase my bulk. At the age of six, they put me in a Sumo training school."

"Did you ever resent having had no say in the matter?" I asked.

"Oh no, on the contrary, I am grateful to them. Thanks to them I am now a famous person. I can have my pick of any girl and I am rich."

"No drawbacks in being so huge?"

"Well, some, I guess. Most of us suffer from insomnia, because our stomachs press on our internal organs, and very few of us live to a ripe old age."

I looked at him. He was huge. His stomach covered everything down to his knees.

I was tempted to ask how he had sex, but I am glad I withstood the temptation.

Whereas interviewing a Sumo wrestler in his locker room certainly was a unique experience, there were certain drawbacks. I had to do it through a Japanese interpreter, who spoke only French, no English. Then I had to translate into Swedish, sometimes simultaneously. For that reason I much preferred to interview Swedes, who came to Tokyo from time to time.

When I heard through the Swedish Embassy that the famous explorer Dr. Sten Bergman, who had just published the best seller, *My Father Was a Cannibal*, was in Tokyo, I immediately asked for an interview.

Dr. Bergman was the first white man to cross New Guinea. In his book he explains how, while exploring the island, he was taken prisoner by a tribe of cannibals. He was just about to be killed and presumably eaten, when a beetle, sacred to the New Guineans, settled on his forehead. This incident saved his life, because the cannibals believed then that *he* was sacred, too. Not only was he set free, but was revered as a holy man, and even adopted by the chief—hence the title of his book.

When I asked Dr. Bergman if he had ever eaten human flesh, he did not answer immediately. I almost regretted the question. Then he sighed and said, "Yes, I had to. It was expected of me as the son of the chief."

"And which part of the human body did you prefer?" I asked.

"Oh," he said. "That's easy to answer. Just like any other man I preferred the breasts and thighs of a young girl."

◆   ◆   ◆

My job at NHK was fun. I had a chance to meet and talk with a lot of interesting people and had the opportunity to learn many things about Japan. An added bonus was that my family and friends could hear my voice from time to time. But in 1959, when I became pregnant again and had a beautiful boy, Mike, I quit my job and became a full time mother.

I was still breast-feeding Mike, when one morning my husband said, "Darling, tonight is the night. I have waited long enough. Tonight I want to make love to you, whether you are ready or not." Then he left for work. And he wasn't kidding; he was dead serious. I had to admit he had been very patient. But I wasn't interested in lovemaking. I wanted to grab what little sleep I could between feedings and I was in some pain. But since I certainly didn't want to become pregnant again so soon, I went to see my gynecologist to have a new diaphragm fitted.

Luckily the doctor spoke English. He examined me and told me what size diaphragm I should get. "Where do I go to get one?" I asked.

"Oh, any department store," he answered. "Go to *Takashimaya*; I'm sure they have them."

So I did. I was a little surprised, that he didn't direct me to a pharmacy or a specialty store for such an intimate item, but this was Japan, and what did I know? At the few cocktail parties, where I met Japanese people, the subject had not come up.

I had been studying Japanese for two years and spoke it fairly well. So I went to Takashimaya department store and found my way to the counter for feminine hygiene. When the sales girl asked me what I was looking for, I realized I didn't know the word for "diaphragm." Strangely enough, that was a word my Japanese tutor hadn't taught me! The sales girl who spoke no English, tried to be very helpful. What was it used for? On which part of the body was it used? Would I please show her?

I was getting more and more frustrated and embarrassed. Finally she handed me paper and pencil. Would I please draw a picture? How do you draw a picture of a diaphragm? I drew a circle, which of course didn't help.

In my frustration I tried to say it in German, Spanish and French, but she didn't understand. Finally, in desperation, I blurted it out in Swedish, *"Pessar!"*

"Oh, pessaruh, dessuneh," she cried, and laughed until tears came into her eyes.

Why the word would be the same in Japanese as in Swedish, I could not figure out. Maybe they both came from Latin? Anyway, I really didn't care. I got my diaphragm and went home. That night I made my husband very happy.

◆   ◆   ◆

When my husband's contract with the CIA was up, he didn't want to renew it. He saw in Japan opportunities to start his own business, which was something he had always wanted, distributing movies for television.

In Japan in the late fifties television was just beginning and it emerged with a bang, providing numerous channels and programs around the clock. In some European countries, Sweden for instance, television started with one channel, which played from five pm to midnight. The result in Japan was, after a short while, there were not enough programs to fill the time slots. That's where George saw his opportunity.

He went to Hollywood and bought boxes of old films for practically nothing. That was before they showed old movies on American television. Since there was such a shortage in Japan, George could name his price. So, he started selling American movies dubbed into Japanese. If you have never seen *I Love Lucy* (pronounced, *"I Rub Rucy,"*) in Japanese, you have missed a great show!

We agreed that I would try to get a job to support the family, while George got his business started. Luckily I found a job as a news writer with the A.F.N., the Armed Forces Network, a radio station run by the American Armed Forces for its military personnel and their families. The program was in English, of course, and strictly news.

In those days, the news was carried by U.P. (United Press), A.P. (Associated Press) and I.N.S. (International News Service.), brought in on big teleprinters, running twenty-four hours a day. My job was to pick out the most important news and re-write it into "spoken language," so that American soldiers, who were not trained announcers, could easily read it.

The news was read for five minutes every hour on the hour. Five minutes on the air was the equivalent of sixty typewritten lines. Producing sixty typewritten lines of the last hour's most important news, every hour on the hour for eight hours a day, was a job that totally overwhelmed me. Besides, I had very little experience in typing.

Sergeant Garcia worked in the newsroom, in what capacity I don't remember, but he was working the same hours I did. One day, when he again saw me getting sick in the waste paper basket, he said, "Why don't you just quit? This job is not for you."

"But I can't. I have to support my family, until my husband starts making some money."

"All right," he answered, "but you have to make some changes. Have you ever heard of carbon copies?"

"Of course I have heard of carbon copies, but I don't understand what you mean," I answered.

"Carbon copies will help you, but first you must change your schedule. Ask for the night shift, midnight till eight o'clock. Nobody listens to the news during the night, or at least not every hour on the hour. You can come in at eleven, or as early as you need, to type your sixty lines of news summary for the midnight newscast. Make seven carbon copies for the remaining ones. Then you sleep for the rest of the night."

I followed his advice. Nobody was the wiser. I kept my job for six months, until my husband's business started to flourish.

Bless you, Sergeant Garcia, wherever you are!

◆   ◆   ◆

Over the years I learned more and more how different George and I really were.

One evening we invited some American friends to one of Tokyo's best restaurants. After an excellent meal with good service we all ordered coffee, except

George who ordered tea. Now, when you order tea in English in Japan, it means black tea. If you want Japanese tea, you use another word, *ocha*. Well, the waiter brought *ocha*, which tastes totally different from English tea and is disliked by most westerners. When George pointed out that he had ordered *tea*, not *ocha*, the waiter said, "So sorry, but the kitchen is closed, so you can't have it."

George was furious, but he didn't show it. However, I noticed the pulsating vein in his forehead and knew what *that* meant. He received the bill and left without paying.

When the waiter tried to stop us, George said," Oh, yes, I'll pay my bill as soon as I get the tea I ordered. Here is my office address. Deliver the tea, and I'll pay the bill."

Then we quickly got into the car and left. Had there just been the two of us, I wouldn't have minded. But this way George embarrassed our guests, and that I found difficult to accept.

Every month for about a year George received the bill at his office, and every month he answered politely that he would pay it, as soon as his tea was delivered. You'd think that one or the other would give up, but I guess neither one of them wanted to loose face. As far as I know, the bill is still unpaid.

Sometimes when I became excited about something I was planning to do and wanted to share it with George, he would answer, "Don't tell me what you are going to do, tell me what you have done." That was often very hurtful, and it was even more so, when he said it our son Mike.

During most of our marriage George was away on business trips. He didn't want me to go with him. He felt I should be staying home with the children. Well, I could see his point. But we *did* have servants and also grandpa, my father-in-law, who loved the kids and was a great babysitter. I missed George very much, but I eventually compensated for his absences by making plenty of friends.

I spent more time with my father-in-law than I did with my husband. I was very fond of him, but he spoke only Russian and mine was never very good. I remember once when I took him to the dentist. He only knew two words in Japanese, *haisara* (ashtray) and *sayonara* (goodbye). *Haisara* he had to learn in order to tell our maid to bring an ashtray; he was the only one who smoked. Trouble was, he got the two words mixed up. So when he left the dentist, he said "*haisara!*"

Grandpa also went with me to see the movie Dr. Zhivago. I had wanted to see it with George; we had read the book together, he in Russian and I in English, but as usual he was away. Grandpa had lived in the Soviet Union during the period the movie depicted. After we got home, we stayed up half the night, while he was telling me so much more about that remarkable period in history.

How I wished, that I had understood Russian better than I did!

◆   ◆   ◆

When Katya was six I took her to Sweden again. We stayed with my sister and her four children, who spoke only Swedish. Katya learned quickly that if she wanted to play with them, she had to do it in Swedish. I am sure this was not always easy, but when I came back after being away for a week, she spoke only Swedish; in fact she refused to speak English to me! I was delighted and from then on we spoke only Swedish to each other.

On the plane back to Japan, when we were a couple of hours from Tokyo, I told her that we had better start speaking English, because Daddy would meet us at the air-port and he spoke no Swedish. But, she didn't want to and greeted her father in Swedish. He wasn't at all pleased, and accused me of having "turned his daughter into a Swede!"

But, later that day he boasted to some of our Swedish friends that his daughter had learned to speak fluent Swedish in only three months. In fact, why didn't they come over to the house to see and hear for themselves?

They did. What my husband hadn't realized though, was by that time our daughter had spent a whole day with her American playmates, speaking nothing but English. So, when asked to speak to our Swedish friends, she spoke only English, not a word of Swedish.

◆   ◆   ◆

After four years in Tokyo and with George's business going well, we decided to move to Yokohama. Yokohama was much prettier than Tokyo, and we rented a large villa overlooking Yokohama Bay. There we could sit on the veranda, watching ships from all over the world coming in to dock. We bought a little motorboat and motored in and out among the ships, saluting the sailors with our drinks at the cocktail hour and frequently greeting them in their own languages. George spoke Russian, German, Czech, and Polish and I, Swedish, German, French and Spanish. And, of course, we both spoke English. It was great fun.

The lives of most of us foreign women were lives of leisure. Even if we had *wanted* to work, we could not have. The Japanese companies would not hire foreign women, and the foreign companies hired only Japanese women for secretarial work, etc. As far as working in positions similar to those our husbands had, that was extremely rare for women at that time, particularly abroad.

There was little to occupy us at home. Servants took care of all household chores. A staff of five was common: cook, maid, nanny, gardener and chauffeur.

So what did we do? We had parties. That was the logical outcome, especially in the international community, for women who didn't work and had plenty of servants. I loved it; still do, but not so George. So, we made a deal. We would accept only every other party. I was disappointed, but better something than nothing.

Frequently, at the parties we *did* attend, after about an hour or so, George started looking at his watch, sometimes shaking it and putting it to his ear. Obviously he wanted to leave. I didn't. I was just getting started. But eventually we left when he wanted to—much too early for me, but what could I do?

When we returned home, I made another deal. Every other party we went to, *I* would decide when to leave. At least I could enjoy every fourth party!

Today, and in the U.S., that kind of life seems extremely extravagant. But life was different then, especially in Japan. First of all, a great number of Japanese people, especially women, needed work after the war. Women, who before the war, would have been married off by their parents, now had to fend for themselves. Their fathers and prospective husbands were gone. Trained only to be housewives and mothers, they eagerly became servants, especially to foreigners. Many cooks had a younger relative, whom they wanted to work with them as a maid or nanny.

If you were a foreigner, a chauffeur was a must. If you wanted to drive anywhere in Tokyo, it was next to impossible to find your way around. Not only were the street names very difficult for a foreigner to read, but also the houses were numbered, not according to their position on the street, but according to when they were built. So there could be a house numbered 172 right next to number 3. Addresses were given to a general area where the policeman on the beat knew where everybody lived. So, when we visited somebody, our chauffeur called our friend's chauffeur and between them, they worked out how to get there.

One day one of my neighbors called, "Kerstin, we are all going to have our children's portraits painted. Mary has found this great portrait painter, *Nakaosan*. He is very good with children—does a portrait in one day. Why don't you have him do Katya and Mike?"

Catherine was, as always, enthusiastic about this new idea. She, Mary and I were among the many American and European expatriates in Yokohama in the sixties. We met for various activities: bridge, tennis, flower arrangements and tea ceremony at the American Club, while our husbands worked for various foreign companies.

I thought the idea of having my children's portraits painted a great one. Christmas was coming up, and what better presents to my husband than their portraits?

Nakaosan, the young artist, was good. He captured our children's likenesses well, and I managed to keep them entertained, so that they sat still. They were only three and eight years old. In fact, Nakaosan was so good, that I decided to have my portrait painted, too. Now we each had a Christmas present for Daddy.

Nakaosan did mine in one day also. It was not quite as successful. The reason was, my children had me to keep them happy while they sat; I had nobody. So I listened to the radio, co-incidentally the day that President Kennedy was killed. Naturally I was sad, and it showed in the portrait.

On Christmas, when my husband opened his presents, he was delighted with the children's portraits. But mine he didn't like at all. "You look so sad," he said. "I don't want to see a sad face every time I look at your portrait."

"But what am I going to do with it?" I asked.

"Give it to your mother. She is nearsighted," he answered. Of course I was disappointed, but I took his advice.

My mother was delighted. She wrote to me, "I have put your beautiful portrait at the foot of my bed. You, Darling, are the first thing I see in the morning, and the last thing before I go to sleep at night."

◆   ◆   ◆

The years went by and whenever I visited my mother, there was my portrait at the foot of her bed.

The day came, when she passed away. Some time after the funeral all of us children gathered to divide her belongings. An appraiser had helped us sort the things into groups: valuable things, not so valuable things and things with nothing but sentimental value. My portrait was in the pile of only sentimental value. We drew lots to decide who would pick first from each pile. My younger brother picked first. He didn't pick my portrait. Then it was my sister's turn. She didn't pick it either. This was getting embarrassing and, I have to admit, I was a little hurt.

Nobody wanted my portrait! First my husband, and now my brother and sister. The only one who had wanted it was my mother, and she was, as my husband had pointed out, nearsighted.

My feelings must have shown on my face, because, when it became my older brother's turn (he and I were very close,) he said "Oh, goody, nobody saw Kerstin's portrait, so I can have it!"

I don't know how much he really wanted it, but his wife made it clear that *she* didn't! Nevertheless, for the next twenty years it hung in their apartment, where I saw it every time I visited.

Not long ago my brother and sister-in-law passed away. Now, my niece owns the portrait. She recently told me that she might give it to my daughter. I am holding my breath to see *her* reaction. I have a sinking feeling that she will react to it just like her father.

◆   ◆   ◆

When we lived in Yokohama, we invited my mother to visit. She had recently become widowed and I felt the trip would be god for her. I was a little worried about her traveling so far all alone at her age. After all, she was seventy!

I didn't want her to worry about not finding me at the airport, so I asked permission to meet her on the tarmac right at the bottom of the stairs. Since she flew with SAS and I knew the ground chief, that was easily arranged. So there I stood, waiting anxiously, when my mother came down, arm in arm with the pilot! And she wasn't even flying first class!

During her stay she spent much time alone with my Russian father-in-law, since George and I both worked. At first I wondered how they would get along. Swedes in general don't like Russians. But my father-in-law was not a *Soviet* Russian. He was born before the revolution and he was not a member of the Communist party.

They couldn't speak to each other, since my father-in-law spoke only Russian, which mother didn't speak. They became good friends though, and had one thing in common; they both had the most wonderful grandchildren in the world, and loved to play with them, each in his/her own language. I believe children can play with their grandparents in any language!

One day I came home earlier than usual and found my mother and my father-in-law sitting on the veranda, talking away! How could they do that? They had no language in common. I sneaked up on them to listen. Mother was speaking

Swedish, my father-in-law Russian. Both of them had turned off their hearing aids!

◆   ◆   ◆

After a while in Yokohama I was getting bored with cocktail parties, ladies' luncheons, and bridge. I wanted to work. Since I had already been teaching Swedish in America, first at Augustana College and later at the Army Language School in Monterey, and had really enjoyed it, I thought, "Why not try to get a teaching job in Yokohama?"

Obviously I couldn't teach in the Japanese school system, but maybe in the American military system? Also, obviously, I couldn't teach any of the languages that I had taught before, Swedish or English. But what about French or Spanish? I spoke both those languages fairly well. The American Armed Forces had high schools for the children of their personnel. They taught Spanish and French, because they followed the curriculum of the stateside schools.

I applied and was accepted. A week later I was teaching French and Spanish at Camp Zama American High School. The assignment was tough at first, since I had never taught children before. I had problems with discipline, especially with the boys. Luckily, those were soon solved, after I confided in the coach, who had become a friend of mine. What he said to them I don't know, but it worked. No more discipline problems for me. I guess coaches have special ways to keep boys in line. Extra push-ups come to mind.

I enjoyed teaching at Zama where, among other things, I was in charge of the Language Laboratory. That was a novelty in the sixties. One day I learned that the American ambassador and his wife (who incidentally spoke Spanish) were coming to visit. They wanted to see how the school worked and to decide, if installing language laboratories in other American high schools in Japan was a good idea.

The laboratory was set up in such a way that the teacher, in this case, I, could listen in on the students when they talked and talk to them, without either of us seeing each other.

I gave some extra earphones to my visitors, and just happened to listen in on Jaime Garcia. He had no difficulties whatsoever in translating an English text into Spanish, and his pronunciation was excellent! My guests were impressed.

Not long after, several language laboratories were installed at other American high schools in Japan.

There were many advantages to teaching at an American military camp. We had PX and Commissary privileges, which meant I could buy anything that was sold in the States, tax-free. In the sixties there were so many things you simply couldn't get in Japan: coffee and children's shoes, for instance. We even bought a brand new Cadillac at the PX. To me this car was luxurious beyond belief. The only car I had owned until then was a used Volkswagen bug.

We took the Cadillac—a very masculine car—with us in 1964, when we moved to Rome, Italy. The Cadillac's story is unique; I think I'll let him tell it himself.

14

The Cadillac's Story

I was big. I was shiny black. I was brand-new—actually newer than brand-new, because I was a 1965-year model in 1964. My interior was silver gray leather and smelled wonderfully rich. The windows opened electronically by pressing a button—no rolling them down with a handle! I was shipped from the States to a U.S. military base in Camp Zama, Japan, where U.S. military personnel could buy me in the P.X.

One day a lady, who taught in the high school for the children of military personnel, came in and bought me. Her husband made big money selling American TV shows to Japanese TV-stations. But he made it in yen, and one was not allowed at that time to take yen out of the country. The high school paid the schoolteacher in M.P.C. (Military Payment Certificate). The soldiers were paid every two weeks, also in M.P.C., but they needed yen for expenses in Japan.

Every other Thursday, which was payday, they stood in long lines before the exchange windows at the various military bases to get yen for their M.P.C. The schoolteacher stood in those lines too, with her husband's yen, often asking somebody at the end of the line, if he would exchange with her rather than wait in line. She had sold her car, she said, and had more yen than she could use. So they changed their money with her, and she got the M.P.C., which she could deposit in her bank account in the States.

Every other Thursday her driver, Wadasan, drove me from one military base after another around Tokyo. Thank God, the schoolteacher didn't drive me! That important task went to a professional chauffeur, who always wore a uniform with gold buttons, and saluted when he held open my door. Only proper, for I was, after all, a Cadillac. Only one other Cadillac stayed on the base, and the general's chauffeur drove it. But I was several years newer, eh, younger.

The schoolteacher sat in the back seat surrounded by hundreds of thousands of yen, all in big bundles.

She told me that she was a little uneasy, when she thought about what would happen, if we were stopped for any reason; what she was doing was definitely illegal. To add to the problem, she also had to get leave from her teaching on the days she went around changing money.

Finally she ran out of excuses. How many Thursdays in a row can the children get sick, or her father-in-law need to be taken to the dentist? But then a new idea struck her. Female problems! As soon as you start talking about female problems to a male boss, she told me, he becomes very considerate and says, "Of course, take time off," and gets embarrassed and finishes the conversation as soon as possible to get rid of you. (Off the record, she has had at least four hysterectomies!)

I had the most fun when the schoolteacher's husband filled me with geishas and we drove out to the airport to pick up American businessmen. Both the men and the geishas loved those rides, particularly in the backseat, where they enjoyed my shiny, new and good-smelling interior. Every other Thursday however, I had to go to one military base after another. Booooring! Except once, when we were caught speeding by the military police. That was fun!

One morning on our way from Camp Zama to Camp Drake, I heard a siren behind us. In the back mirror I saw flashing red lights: the M.P! The schoolteacher quickly threw her coat over the bundles of yen and tried to look innocent. Her heart was beating so hard I could hear it. I was sure the police could, too. She was wet all through from perspiration. Even my beautiful upholstery got wet. I wondered what she was going to say, when the policeman came up to the window. He was very polite.

"Excuse me," he said to Wadasan "may I please see your driver's license? You are going too fast."

A red-faced Wadasan got a speeding ticket and apologized profusely. The schoolteacher was so relieved she almost kissed him. A speeding ticket! She had never been so happy over a speeding ticket in her life. Compared to prison for currency violation, a speeding ticket was nothing to worry about. A few days later she told me she had been called in to see the principal of the school.

"Mrs. Shirokow, didn't you call in sick last Thursday?" he asked.

"Yes," she answered, "I had some female trouble."

"I see," he said. "Then how come that you were on your way to Camp Drake that day?"

How did he know that I was in Camp Drake? she thought. Then she remembered: the speeding ticket!

"Well," she said, "I was on my way to the hospital."

"Oh, I see," he said, "well, I just have to check up on things; I hope you understand."

Luckily, there *was* a hospital in Camp Drake. Who knows whether it had a female clinic?

◆   ◆   ◆

After two years in the Orient came a big adventure. I went to Rome on a ship. On board I was a great success and much admired. The sailors took turns pretending to drive me, and they loved pressing the buttons to make the windows go up and down. They played with me so much, they wore me out. My battery went dead.

When we arrived in Ostia, Rome's port town, I was taken to a place called customs. The garages were too small, so I was left out in the rain. I was cold, wet and miserable. Because my battery was dead, the windows wouldn't close, so I was soaked through inside as well. My back seat was so wet that toadstools began to grow. Day and night I waited for the schoolteacher to come and rescue me. Had she totally abandoned me?

She had to wait for a notification that the Cadillac had arrived in customs. She came and saw me standing outside the garage without license plates, the windows open, and the battery dead. A used car without license plates was not allowed to enter Italy, so I was there illegally.

In her rather poor Italian she asked, "What am I supposed to do?" After a lot of talking and gesticulating and shrugging of shoulders, she went see *il commandatore* Othello who couldn't help me, but another gentleman, *il signor* Amletto, suggested she call the Japanese embassy. (Both of their mothers must have been Shakespeare fans.) Maybe they could provide the license plates for me.

Before she left, she talked to a bunch of people about getting my battery out and recharged, so my windows could be closed. Apparently that was not easy, because the battery, too, was in Italy illegally. While she was gone, some guy came, opened my hood, stuck his hand in and took my battery. The nerve of him! Can you imagine? He wasn't even a mechanic; I could tell by the clumsy way he handled me. I felt like running him over. But how could I? I couldn't even get started.

After awhile he came back. He had recharged the battery. How did *he* get it out, when the schoolteacher had so many problems? He simply didn't bother about any customs. He just put my battery in his toolbox, took it out, had it recharged, took it back and put it in me; against regulations of course, but no one was the wiser. Now at least the windows could be closed and I wouldn't get wet inside. I still didn't have my license plates, and had to be kept in customs. I wondered for how long?

During the next couple of months the schoolteacher wrote, called, and visited the Japanese embassy innumerable times. She received very polite answers to her letters, very polite returns of her phone calls and very polite assurances when she visited, but no license plates.

One day, the schoolteacher told me, while she was out walking in the neighborhood, she passed a large villa, flying the Japanese flag. It was the Japanese ambassador's residence. Although she knew very well, it was not the proper thing to do, she went up to the residence and pressed the doorbell.

A Japanese butler opened the door. In her best Japanese, she asked if she could see the ambassador. The butler looked at her condescendingly.

"Do you have an appointment?"

"I don't, but it is important and it will only take a couple of minutes."

"I am so sorry, but it is impossible to see the ambassador without an appointment."

While they stood there talking, the ambassador walked by.

"Your Excellency," she called in Japanese.

He stopped, turned around, and was no doubt surprised to hear a westerner speaking Japanese. "Won't you please come in?" he said pleasantly.

"Thank you," she answered. Then he asked the butler to serve tea. While drinking the delicious Japanese tea, she explained her difficulties with the Japanese embassy.

"I am not at all surprised," the ambassador answered. "Most of the people there are utterly incompetent."

"But Your Excellency, what am I to do? I have to get my car out."

"Do you have any photographs of the license plates?" he asked.

"I think so."

"Have new license plates made then, and put them on."

So she went to a sign maker with the photographs and asked him to copy the license plates, but he flatly refused. The car could have been stolen, he said, and he didn't want to have anything to do with it. When she explained to him, that the Japanese government had kept the license plates, and that the Japanese Ambassador had told her to have them copied he said, "The Japanese Ambassador, eh? No shit!" and pretended to be very impressed. Discouraged, she returned home and told Mario, our chauffeur, what had happened.

"But I can copy the plates, *Signora*," he said.

Finally the schoolteacher came back to see me with some strange-looking license plates, which she put on me. They were not as nice as my previous ones. They looked homemade somehow, but thanks to them I got out of customs, and was I glad!

With these homemade plates they could park me anywhere in Rome. When *i carabinieri* (traffic police men) came to give me a parking ticket and started to write down the numbers on the license plates, they were stumped. They couldn't copy the Japanese characters!

My carefree Roman holiday did not last. After a terrible accident on the Autostrada del Sole (not my fault and no passengers were hurt), I became a total wreck. I had to be *towed* back to Rome!

For the next couple of years I stood in the schoolteacher's garden, where her children played house in me on my once beautiful silver-gray upholstery. I was finally sold to a movie company for two hundred dollars. They needed a car that could be pushed off a pier and explode in the ocean. The schoolteacher told me my end would come in a blaze of glory. What a way to go, captured on film for others to enjoy for years to come!

15

Rome

The Cadillac wasn't the only one who had problems when arriving in Rome. So did I, mainly because I didn't speak Italian. The kids managed all right. They went to an international school with children from many different countries and everybody was taught in English. They also learned Italian from the neighbor's children, with whom they played. My husband almost immediately returned to Japan on business, and I was left to handle the every day chores in a language I didn't know.

One day, after having eaten out for a week, I decided it was time for me to start cooking, so we could eat at home. So, I ventured out grocery shopping. Chicken and rice was what I had planned for dinner. I had looked up the word for chicken (pollo), which I proudly said in the grocery store.

"Si, Signora," said the butcher and handed me a chicken: feathers, feet, head and all. I changed my mind and bought ground meat. So what, the kids liked hamburgers. But I still needed salt. All the other things I could point at, but salt was nowhere to be found.

I looked up the words, *"Dove e il sale?"* (Where is the salt?)

Apparently I pronounced them correctly, because an incomprehensible stream of Italian words, a big smile and lots of gestures answered me. But, no salt. I went to five different stores, said the same phrase, got the same answer; still no salt. I realized that they were all telling me something about *sale,* but what? I gave up, called my friend Bianca and asked her," How come all the grocery stores in Rome are out of salt?" She laughed and said that in Italy salt was sold at the tobacconist's.

"Why at the tobacconist's?" I asked.

She didn't know, and it really didn't matter. I found a tobacconist, and sure enough, they had salt. (Later I learned that salt, as well as tobacco, was a government concession, controlled and taxed by the government.)

With my salt, ground meat and other provisions I went home and cooked hamburgers for dinner.

◆   ◆   ◆

I was very fortunate to have in Rome a friend from my student years in Stockholm, Bianca Bonicatti. Years earlier when we were both in our twenties, Bianca had found herself in a very difficult situation. She had fallen in love with a young Swedish man she had met on a train and had followed him to Stockholm, where they lived together. Bianca's parents were scandalized and refused to have a anything to do with her. Then the young man took ill, and they both moved into his parents' home.

When the young man suddenly died, his parents, who hadn't liked Bianca living with their son in the first place, asked her to leave. That's when I first met her at the University Center for Foreign Students. She was totally distraught.

"I have nowhere to live, no money, and I don't speak Swedish nor English."

Luckily we could communicate in French. "You can stay with me," I said, "but I do think you should call you parents, explain everything and ask their forgiveness. I'm sure they will welcome you back." We talked through the night, and I finally persuaded her to make the call.

All that happened a long time ago. Bianca eventually married *Marquese* Paolo Ludovici. She never forgot her Swedish boy friend though, and for years she kept his photograph under her bed. She also never forgot that I had helped her. She found a villa for us to rent, a car for us to buy and a couple to help in the household. Because she was very much a society lady, Bianca told all her friends that they should invite "Cristina e Giorgo" to their parties. If they didn't, she would not invite them to hers!

I hired the couple Bianca had found, Mario and Iolanda Barcarolli, to take care of the household. Mario was the chauffeur and Iolanda the cook. I could not communicate with them at first, but we used a lot of gestures, which Italians are used to anyway, and, little by little, my Italian improved.

Mario drove me where I wanted to go; I gave him a list (in Italian!) of the things I wanted him to buy, the errands I wanted him to do and when and where he should pick me up. It worked for quite awhile.

Then one day, when he came to pick me up, he hadn't done a single errand on the list, nor bought any of the things. Naturally I was annoyed and asked him why. He didn't answer, just looked embarrassed. That evening Iolanda came in and wanted to talk to me. She explained that Mario was sorry about what had happened that morning, but he didn't know how to read.

"Mario doesn't know how to read?" I asked. "But I have given him lists of what to do for months, and he always did it all," I said, surprised. "How could he have done that, if he couldn't read?

"*Signora,* until today you always gave him the list before you left. He took it to me, I read it to him and he memorized it. This time you gave it to him in the car."

◆   ◆   ◆

As time went by, my Italian improved, and after about six months I could make myself completely understood. Or so I thought. My daughter's birthday was coming up and I asked Iolanda to make a cake, decorated with lots of strawberries, Katya's favorite. Imagine my surprise when Iolanda carried it in, candles and all, but instead of strawberries it was covered with brown beans! Strawberries in Italian is *fragole*; beans is *fagioli*. I had mixed them up. When I told Yolanda that she should have understood that I had made a mistake (whoever would decorate a cake with beans!) she answered," Ah, *Signora*, if you only knew, how many strange things you have asked me to do! This was nothing!"

◆   ◆   ◆

Everything in Rome was great: its history, art, architecture, food and last, but not least, definitely not least, the men! Roman men really know how to treat a woman. They make you feel like a princess. It doesn't matter, if you are married or not, or if *they* are married. They shower you with compliments so outrageous that you can't possibly believe them, but they are wonderful to hear nevertheless. What a contrast to the stiff, reserved Swedish men I knew, who don't know how to give a compliment, even if they would ever want to!

George traveled a great deal during those years, and I was often the only non-Italian woman in our group of friends, made up mostly of couples. Invariably at parties most of the husbands would surround me, talk to me, and flirt with me and totally ignore their wives. Of course I loved all the attention, but sometimes wondered how the wives felt about it.

Every Sunday night, which was the servants' night off, about eight couples, all Bianca's friends and my husband and I went out for dinner. Except, since my husband often was away, I frequently went by myself.

One evening, as we were having dinner, I sat between Paolo and Leonardo, with their wives sitting opposite us.

All of a sudden I felt Paolo's hand on my knee under the table. I was so surprised I didn't know what to do, and before I had time to object, I felt Leonardo's hand on my other knee. Both hands were slowly moving upwards! All the while, we were all talking with their wives facing us.

This was too much and, I thought, too funny to ignore! So, taking action, I lightly caressed Paolo's hand on my one knee and then Leonardo's on my other. Then I took Paolo's hand and put it on Leonardo's and, very slowly, placed first one of my hands on the table and then the other, while sweetly smiling at them both.

It took them a moment before they realized, that *they* were holding hands on *my* knee! After that they concentrated on the ladies on their other side.

One day I asked Bianca, "Doesn't it bother you and the other wives, that so much attention is given me and not to you?"

"Oh, Cristina," she answered, "you don't understand. Our husbands have already flirted with all of us; you are new and often alone. That excites them. And some of that excitement spills over onto us. It would be boring for everyone if you were not here."

◆   ◆   ◆

When George *was* home we traveled with the children to many places in Italy and Greece. Two places stand out in my memory; Pompeii in Italy and Olympia in Greece.

Before Pompeii was destroyed in the year 79 by a volcanic eruption of Vesuvius, it was the pleasure city of the emperors. Now tourists can visit the ruins of the pleasure houses, which bear signs indicating the type of pleasure offered. Some were considered too risqué for women to visit, so we tourists were separated according to gender. Men could visit all the houses, but at some, women were not allowed.

Our ten-year-old daughter Katya was extremely annoyed that she couldn't visit a house, which her five-year-old brother Mike was allowed to see!

It depicted the blindfolded Goddess of Justice, holding a scale. On one side were all the riches in the world, on the other an enormous penis. The penis weighed more.

When Mike came back, Katya eagerly asked: "Mike, what was it? What did you see?"

"Oh, Katya," he answered," You should have seen it! It was the hugest pee-pee I have ever seen!"

In Olympia in Greece we visited the stadium where the Olympic games were started in ancient times. What a thrill to follow in the footsteps around the same track where the very first Olympians had run!

◆   ◆   ◆

My mother had visited Italy as a young girl with her grandmother, but they never went to Rome. So she was delighted when we invited her for a visit. One phrase she still remembered from that time was, "Buena sera," (good evening) and she loved to say it, morning, noon and night.

Piazza Navona, a beautiful place with the great Bernini fountains, was one of our favorite places. One day we had just finished a long, leisurely luncheon, and my mother had drunk *two* glasses of wine instead of her usual one. She was in a great mood. All of a sudden she asked, "Kerstin, have you ever had an orgasm?"

I was speechless. My *mother* was asking me, if I had ever had an orgasm!

"Mother," I stuttered, "what a question! Of course I have. George and I have a good marriage, and our sex life is great. Why do you ask such a question?"

"Well, you see, I have never had one."

I was stunned.

"You never … well, I never would have thought that of Father! That he was so selfish and uncaring!"

My mother interrupted me.

"No, no, don't blame your father. He didn't know that women could enjoy sex. Men didn't know that in those days, and most women didn't expect to, either."

"Men didn't know? Women didn't expect to?" I was flabbergasted. "But Mother, if that is so, how come you even know what an orgasm *is*?

"I have read about it in the books you have lent me."

Naturally, I told George about the conversation. A few days later we passed my mother sitting in the living room, reading. George said, "Look at your mother, she is reading a sexy part."

"How do you know?"

"Look at the red flushes on her cheeks."

My mother was oblivious to us. She had turned off her hearing aid.

◆   ◆   ◆

My dear friend Bianca had done so many things to help my family and me settle in Rome, that when she called me one day to say she had a favor to ask, I was more than happy to comply.

"I'll do anything I can for you, Bianca, anything at all. Tell me what it is."

"Well, I want to ask you something, but I am a little embarrassed to do it," she answered.

"Come on, Bianca, we have been friends for a long time. You know you can ask me anything," I said.

"All right," she said. "Would you buy a diaphragm for me when you get to Sweden. But please don't tell anybody I asked you."

In the week before my departure from Rome to Stockholm, Anna, Francesca, Paola and Laura, all Italian friends of mine, all in their late thirties and with two or three children each, had called me with the same, confidential request.

The reason behind it was that in Italy in the sixties all means of birth control were strictly forbidden by the Catholic Church and impossible to get.

I explained to my friends that diaphragms come in many sizes with no such thing as "one size fits all." They were surprised but not dissuaded.

"Just get the same size you have," they said. "Better something than nothing."

So I agreed. In Stockholm I went to one of the many shops run by a government organization, whose name translates The *Institute for Information on Sexual Matters*. I asked the sales lady for five diaphragms. She looked surprised but, showing typical Swedish reserve, said nothing at first. Finally she asked, "Excuse me, but why do you need *five*?"

Not being able to resist I said, "Oh, they wear out you know, and where I live, you can't get them. I certainly don't want to risk being without."

I left the store chuckling at the incredulous expression on her face. So far, the shopping for my Italian friends had been quite amusing, and I was determined to have some more fun when I returned to Rome. I decided to have a ladies luncheon party and invited my five friends. At each place setting was a party favor in a pretty little box. When the dessert was served, I suggested that they open their presents. I wish I had a picture of the looks on their faces, when they opened their boxes and realized that they all received the same party favor! They showed surprise, delight, relief, but also embarrassment and even anger, all mixed together. After all, they had asked me not to tell anyone. We all had a good laugh, and they went home, presumably to try out their new party favors.

Within a year, I was invited to three baby showers.
I was right; one size doesn't fit all!

◆   ◆   ◆

Years later, well after my divorce from George, my friend Bob and I were driving around in Umbria, Italy, when I saw a sign for Todi, an old historic town. I remembered that Mario and Iolanda had moved there after we left Rome. I wondered if they still lived there. Their name was in the telephone directory, so I called the number. Iolanda answered.

"*Buon giorno*, Iolanda," I said, "I am Cristina Shirokow. You and Mario worked for my family in Rome a long time ago. Do you remember me?"

"Remember you? Of course, Signora. I have never forgotten you. How are Signor Shirokow, Katya and Mike and *il nonno* (grandpa)?"

"We are all fine, Iolanda. We are driving near Todi, and we would like to come and see you. *Va bene* (OK)?"

"*Si, Signora,* please come. We would love to see you."

"Thank you. But, Iolanda, no need to call me '*Signora.*' You are not working for me anymore. Call me Cristina."

"Oh no, *Signora*, I can't do that. It would not be proper!"

She gave me the directions and an hour later we met them at their lovely house, surrounded by olive trees. When they saw Bob, they were very surprised. I had forgotten to tell them, that "*Signor*" Shirokow had been replaced!

When we came into their living room, we saw two framed photographs on the mantelpiece: Katya at age thirteen and Mike at age eight. They had kept them all those years! Then Iolanda took me into the kitchen, and showed me her washing machine. "Do you recognize it, *Signora*?" When I shook my head, she said, "It was yours in Rome. You gave it to me when you left. It still works fine, and all my friends are envious of me for having an *American* washing machine!"

An American washing machine that I had bought at the Yokohama P.X in Japan over twenty years ago!

Shortly before we left, I asked Mario to please call and make reservations at a hotel, where we could spend the night. He said, "sure," went out into the garden, and asked his daughter to look up the number for him. Why didn't he do that himself? After a while I understood. Mario still didn't know how to read.

16

The Pompeian Court

The Pompeian Court

One day George came home and said, "I have a surprise for you. I have bought a house for us in California."

I was surprised and a little annoyed that he had made such an important decision without asking me. Still, I liked the pictures he showed to me of a ten-room villa, sitting on seven acres, beautifully landscaped. In the center of the courtyard there was a Roman atrium with a fountain. There were servants' quarters, a guest cottage, chauffeur's cottage, a two-car garage and a tennis court. A well-known architect had designed it around 1917.

Its name was "The Pompeiian Court," located in Montecito, wherever that was.

The year was 1967, and we had now been living in Rome for three years. I was very happy there; I loved Italy and I loved the Italians, especially the men, but we had been talking about moving to the States for the children's sake. We felt they needed roots somewhere.

This decision became clear to me one day when the head master of the International School in Rome called me and said, "Mrs. Shirokow, I think you should know about a conversation I had with your son today. I asked him, which flag he wanted to carry during the United Nations' Day parade tomorrow. He said he didn't know. So I asked: "Where is your father from?"

"The Soviet Union."

"And your mother?"

"From Sweden."

"Oh, well, where were you born?"

"In Japan."

"So I let him carry the United Nations' flag."

George and I decided to return to the States and make our children Americans. After all, we had met in America, our daughter was born there and we were all American citizens.

And now my husband had bought a house in a place I had never seen and never even heard of!

The lady who had lived there had died, and the house now belonged to her daughters, who lived in New York and wanted to sell it. The estate had been on the market for some time. My husband offered $130,000 dollars, which made the real estate agent laugh, because it was so low. Six months later his offer was accepted and we left Italy for California.

Shortly before our departure some friends hosted a farewell party for us at the Cavalieri Hilton in Rome. The manager, a friend of ours, was invited, too. When he heard we were moving to Montecito, he said, "I have heard of that place. In fact, there is a guest here at the hotel that I think is from there. I believe he is in the bar." And that's how we met John Ireland, the movie actor.

I lived in The Pompeian Court until 1981. Many were the parties that took place there, especially after 1975, when my husband and I divorced. I let benefit organizations use The Pompeian Court for fundraisers. One was for an acquaintance who was running for county supervisor; seven hundred people showed up.

That same day I picked up my sister from Sweden at the Los Angeles airport. The trip was a long one for her and she was tired. On the way home in the car she said, "Now, Kerstin, knowing you, you have probably planned a party for me. But please wait at least a week. I am very tired, and I'd like to practice my English a little first."

I didn't know what to say, or *how* to say, that that very night, she would meet seven hundred of my closest friends!

There were fundraisers and parties for The Lobero Theater, The Art Museum and Alliance Française. In addition to being helpful to all these organizations, the agreement meant a great deal to me personally. Being recently divorced, I was living on a limited income, so this was a good way for me to entertain without spending a lot of money.

I told all my friends who were party-givers and who were involved in fundraisers,

"You may use my house any time as long as you have the house cleaned before and after the party, leave all flower arrangements and opened bottles of wine and liquor and let me invite a few of my friends."

The arrangement turned out to be great for everybody concerned. Even so, keeping the house was getting increasingly difficult for me. Taxes had to be paid; with over seven acres I needed a full time gardener, and repairs were urgently needed. After all, the house was almost sixty years old.

Once when I came home from a party at a fancy home and told my teen-age son Mike that there was a waterfall as a decoration in one of the rooms, he answered, "Big deal! We have a waterfall in the library every time it rains!"

Unfortunately, he was right.

I made some extra money by renting out anything I could: the servants' quarters, the guest cottage and the chauffeur's cottage. I also gave lessons in any language I could think of.

When I heard of two ladies, who were going to the Soviet Union, I offered to give them Russian lessons. My Russian wasn't very good, but it was better than theirs. My daughter, who spoke Russian much better than I, said, "How can you do that, Mama? Your Russian isn't good enough! You'll probably teach them to say *niet* (no) instead of *da* (yes), and they will never be heard of again!"

I also taught French to a young painter, Andrea Andreoli. My fee was fifteen dollars an hour; and after a couple of months he asked me if I could teach him for free, in return for one of his paintings. I told him I would like to, but I needed the money for groceries. One of his paintings is now hanging in a luxury hotel in Santa Barbara. I was told he got five thousand dollars for it!

Finally I sold The Pompeian Court. The bank had urged me to do that for some time, but I was hesitant. My children had grown up there (although they were now in college), and the house was my security blanket. My hesitation paid off. I sold it for over a million dollars. My friends told me I had been very smart to wait until the price had peaked. Smart? What did I know about real estate prices? I just kept it, until I *had* to sell. But I kept the tennis court and part of the property, on which I built a new, much smaller house.

The Pompeian Court has had several owners over the years. One was a script-writer from Hollywood. He often had dancing parties on the terrace; and, from the balcony in my new house, I could hear the music. Once I saw them dancing, and when I looked through my binoculars, I saw they were all men!

A couple of years ago I received an invitation in the mail for a cocktail dance benefit for the Lobero Theater. It was at a private house in Montecito. I called my friend Bob and asked, if he wanted to go. He said, "yes," and asked me, "Where is it?"

"Let me check," I said, and looked at the address on the invitation. It was 319 San Ysidro Road, the address of my old house, The Pompeiian Court! We went, the first time for me in almost twenty years.

Dancing in the big living room, filled with so many memories of other parties, children's birthday parties, graduation parties, anniversaries and benefits was an odd feeling. The house looked pretty much as I remembered, although parts of the house had been extensively renovated. Millions must have been spent on the renovation.

I recently heard it was sold for nine million dollars.

17

The Fuller Brush Man

One morning, while still living in the Pompeian Court, I heard a cheerful voice outside my kitchen window, "*Buon giorno, Signora.*"

I looked up and saw a good-looking man with glittering black eyes. He had a smile, which was both appreciative and sensual, such as most Italian men have, when they see a woman.

This was incredible! I had recently returned to the States after three years in Rome, and how I missed it! I suffered from *mal d'Italia* as the Italians call it. That is homesickness for Italy. I don't know if it is possible for a Swedish girl in Santa Barbara, California, to be homesick for Italy, but I was. I longed for the Italian sun, which warmed me inside and out, turning my body golden brown, for the Mediterranean, which was warm but still refreshing, for all the art and history which surrounded me twenty-four hours a day; for the delicious food in the happy intimate restaurants, where everybody tasted everybody else's food, and "la mamma" cooked and sang in the kitchen.

But most of all, I missed the Italian men. They had made me feel like the most wonderful woman in the world. Of course I realized, that their compliments were exaggerated, but still great to hear. A man at a cocktail party, whom I had known for about five minutes, whispered, "Signora, come into the garden and let the roses smell you!" No American has ever said that to me and maybe that is just as well. Or the taxi driver who, when we arrived, jumped over the wall into somebody else's garden, stole a rose, gave it to me, kissed my hand, overcharged me and drove off. How can you help not liking such people?

And now there was a real, live Italian outside my kitchen window!

"*Avanti,*" I called. "Come in, come in!"

"But you speak Italian," he said with great delight. I was just as delighted to be able to speak Italian, this most musical of languages. to this handsome young man. It is probably no accident that so many operas are written in Italian.

He said that his name was Paolo Concetti, and he was a Fuller Brush man. Did I need any brushes? He had all kinds of brushes: brooms, scrub brushes, hairbrushes, nail brushes, brushes for walls, ceilings and terraces. He talked and gestured and got all excited over these wonderful brushes he had.

I didn't hear a word he said. I only sat and listened to the beautiful Roman Italian he spoke and looked at his gestures, which included the whole universe. No car salesman could have been more enthusiastic over the qualities of his products. These were the Rolls Royces of brushes.

When he stopped for a second, I asked, "Would you like a cup of coffee?" First he hesitated, but when I said, "espresso," he accepted with delight.

We drank coffee and talked about everything and anything at all. It was as if the Italian sun and warmth had entered my November-gray kitchen.

But finally he had to leave, of course. Did I need any brushes? You bet I did! I ordered brushes of all imaginable kinds. For each brush I chose, Paolo gave a description of all its marvelous qualities and expressed his admiration for my good choice. Good choice? What did I care about the brushes? All I wanted was to meet him again! He said that he would deliver the brushes in a week.

On the seventh day I had everything ready for the arrival of the brushes *and* Signor Concetti. The kitchen was spotless, the espresso ready, *Oh, Sole Mio* on the stereo and the phone off the hook. I had been to the beauty parlor. My hair was perfect and I had a manicure and a pedicure too, just in case. I didn't know what time he would come, but I started to wait at ten o'clock. At eleven thirty the doorbell rang. I opened the door. There stood a fat lady with a sullen kid.

She said in a heavy Brooklynese, "My hubby told me to give you these brushes you ordered."

18

Bilingual Proposition

Two things, which I had always wanted but never received when I was married, were a mink coat and a trip to South America. A mink coat in California is kind of silly, but when I lived in Sweden, it had been a status symbol (and also very useful in the winter). I remember how much my mother always had wanted one, but my father could never afford it. My aunt Elsa, of course, had one (probably a gift from an admirer).

So, as soon as my divorce was settled and the house sold, I felt rich in my own right and bought a mink coat. The fur is still hanging in the closet and looks like new. I have worn it about ten times in almost thirty years. The thought never occurred to me to invest the money or to save it, at least not then.

As far as going to South America was concerned, I was lucky to have friends in many South American countries. The first friend I visited was the Finnish ambassador to Brazil. We became friends in Tokyo, where he was first secretary at the Finnish legation when I lived there with my family.

I was met at the airport of the capital Brazilia by a chauffeur of the Finnish Embassy and driven in a Mercedes carrying the Finnish flag to the ambassador's residence. After staying there for a few days I continued to Buenos Aires. On the way I stopped for a day to see the Iguazu Falls, on the border between Brazil, Paraguay and Argentina. Iguazu Falls, right in the middle of the rain forest, is one of the largest waterfalls in the world. I booked a room in the Iguazu Hotel, a big pink palace in the jungle. Awesome in its solitude, it made me feel lonely, sitting all by myself in the huge dining room.

As I ordered dinner and began my entree, a waiter came over with a bottle of wine, compliments of three gentlemen, who sat at a nearby table. I accepted. Why not? I raised my glass to thank them. In fact, I had noticed them and actually been eavesdropping on them for quite awhile. They had a certain air about them and were perfectly at ease. They seemed to be about fifty, tall, blond, quite good-looking, and spoke German. I understood fairly well, what they were saying, having studied German in high school. The topic of their conversation was *I*!

"Is she German?"

"Absolutely not!"

"American?"

"Probably not. An American woman her age would not travel alone in such an out-of-the-way place."

They decided I was English or Scandinavian, not a bad guess. Now I didn't feel lonely anymore. With the wine and the friendly German gentlemen, things were looking up. After awhile one of them came over and asked in good English, if I wanted to join them at their table for coffee. Again, why not?

They all spoke English to me, but German among themselves. They spoke no Spanish and, since I did, they asked me to give the musicians their requests. Around midnight the music stopped, but my German friends were in no mood to go to sleep. So they asked me to invite the musicians to come up to their suite to continue to play. The musicians accepted for a fee. Of course, I was invited, too.

They had a grand suite: three bedrooms, a living room and a bar. We talked, joked, danced and drank. We had a great time, and the musicians played on. I did not tell them that I spoke German and pretended that I did not understand, when they talked among themselves. And what did they talk about? They were discussing who would take me to bed!

Here was a situation that never had occurred to me. How naïve and foolish of me to go with three gentlemen, whom I had known for only a couple of hours, to their room in the middle of the night in a hotel in the middle of the jungle in Brazil! I had obviously learnt nothing from my previous experiences with men! My mother would have turned over in her grave, and my daughter would never believe I could be so stupid!

While all this went through my head, my German "friends" were having quite a discussion. One said, "I should have her, because I saw her first." Another said, "No, I should, since I bought her the wine," and the third said, "You are both wrong. She is mine, because I speak the best English."

About then the musicians wanted to leave. The Germans gave me money and I paid the musicians. Then I turned around and said in my best German,

"*Meine Herren, danke schön*; it has been a wonderful evening, but now it is time for me to go to bed, <u>alone</u>. *Auf Wiedersehen.*" Smiling, I left with the musicians.

I did not look back, which was a shame, for the looks on their faces must have been a priceless thing to remember.

19

An Unforgettable Man

After a few days with friends in Buenos Aires I flew to Brasilia, continuing to New York and Los Angeles.

That's when I saw him, at the airport in Brasilia.

You couldn't help noticing him. He truly stood out: tall, with broad shoulders and dark wavy hair turning a little gray at the temples.

"Oh, I hope he, too, is going to New York," I silently wished.

He wore blue jeans that fit perfectly and the kind of sports jacket I just love, with suede patches on the elbows, leather buttons and a slit in the back. He was a little ahead of me in line going to the New York lounge.

As I was admiring his buns, perfectly shaped and just the right size, a beautiful blond woman came running, calling "Bill, Bill!" He turned around, and I saw the most dazzling smile. As he passed me, I inhaled a whiff of great-smelling eau-de cologne, Gucci Envy, I think. He opened his arms and they embraced; the longest and most romantic embrace I have ever witnessed or experienced, in real life or in the movies. They practically melted into each other.

So, I boarded the plane, disappointed, sure, but what could I do about it? Some of them do get away!

After I found my seat, I looked around, but I couldn't see him. Maybe he was going first class? I tried not to think about him, but the task was difficult. The flight attendant happened to be Swedish, so I asked her, "Could I just peek into first class?"

"Yes, but you can't go in."

So I peeked. He was there all right, sound asleep. It was only eleven o'clock in the morning, so he obviously hadn't had much sleep the night before! The beautiful blond probably hadn't either. I went back to my tourist class seat and followed his example.

When we arrived in New York, where I had a four-hour layover before leaving for Los Angeles, I saw him again! I couldn't believe my eyes! There he was in the arrival lounge in an embrace if possible even *more* all-consuming than the one in Brazilia, with a beautiful woman, a brunette this time. So this was what he had rested up for on the plane! While I waited for a taxi, I saw him getting into one and I heard him say, "The Pierre, please." That was that. I obviously wouldn't see him again.

I was wrong. As I boarded my plane for L.A., there he was again, saying a tender farewell to the brunette. I looked for him on the plane, but couldn't see him. This time I didn't have a chance to check first class.

When we landed in L.A., I was met by a friend and forgot all about Bill. But at the baggage claim I saw him again, warmly talking to a nice-looking woman with two children, obviously theirs. I couldn't resist, so I positioned myself next to him while waiting for my luggage and said quietly, "My, what an operator you are!"

He looked up, a little startled at first, then, looking around to see if his wife was within hearing distance, smiled and put his finger to his lips. I later told my friend about him, and he agreed, with a little bit of envy I think, that Bill was quite an operator.

Over the years I have thought about Bill from time to time, wondering how he was managing all his women. I am sure, that I had witnessed only a fraction of them. Did his wife ever find out? Did the blonde and the brunette find out about the wife and about each other?

I guess I'll never know.

20

My Mother's Blind Ladies

Mother's last visit was to Santa Barbara, when she was seventy-eight years old. At a party I gave in her honor, one of the male guests asked, "Well, Mrs. Hård af Segerstad, do you have any more pretty daughters at home?"

A typical male flattering comment, which didn't really merit an answer other than a smile. But my mother took it as a factual question, which required a factual answer. She thought for a moment and then said, "Well, Kerstin's sister is prettier, but Kerstin has more sex-appeal."

That from my *mother!*

When she left from Los Angeles to go back to Sweden, I asked the SAS ground chief, who was friend if mine, if there were any empty seats in first class. My mother had a tourist class ticket; it never entered her head to go first class. She had never done that. My friend said he'd see what he could do.

I waited to wave goodbye. Just before they closed the door, there was my mother shouting *"Första klass, första klass,"* with a huge smile on her face.

My Mother's Blind Ladies

She passed away a few months later.

I went to Sweden for the funeral; the first time I went back with *sadness* in my heart.

While I was sitting in church and after the family and friends had said their final "good-byes," seven old ladies walked up to the coffin. They walked in a row, holding hands. Each of them stopped for a moment, curtsied, and placed a red rose on the coffin. The scene was like a painting by Breughel.

"Who are they?" I asked my brothers and sister, but nobody knew.

All of a sudden it came to me! They must be my mother's "blind ladies!" Every Tuesday as far back as I can remember, from the time I was a little girl, Mother read to the blind ladies. This was in my little hometown in Sweden, before The Braille Institute, The Recording for the Blind or any social help at all had been developed for the blind—when people who were blind were called *blind*, and not *visually impaired.* What a voluminous number of books my mother must have read to them every week for over thirty years!

And now they were saying goodbye to her!

The next day I decided to go to them and thank them for their tribute to my mother. I called and they invited me for tea. When I arrived at their apartment, there was the most beautiful tea table I have ever seen: exquisite cups and saucers, beautiful silver, linen napkins and flowers beautifully arranged.

They served delicious cookies and cakes and little finger sandwiches so effortlessly, it was impossible to believe they couldn't see.

We sat down and when they had served the tea, (not a drop was spilled!) came the greatest surprise of all. They started asking me questions.

"How is your father-in-law? Is he still speaking only Russian, or has he learned some English yet?" asked one of the ladies in a very gentle voice.

How did they know I had a Russian father-in-law who couldn't speak English?

"Do your children still speak Japanese, or have they forgotten it?" asked another.

How did they know we had lived in Japan?

"Was it hard to drive again after you employed chauffeurs for ten years?"

"Yes, it certainly was, especially on the freeways. As a matter of fact, I have had quite a few minor accidents. But how do you know about my chauffeurs?"

They just smiled. They seemed to know everything about my life, and yet we had just met. I was absolutely flabbergasted. They obviously must have enjoyed my consternation and puzzlement, for they kept on asking questions referring to my life. It was almost as if they were showing off their knowledge of what my family and I had done. Finally I had to ask how they knew so much about me. I mean, it isn't as if I were famous or anything. When they told me, I realized that I should have guessed it. My mother, bless her!

Whenever my mother came back from visiting me, (in Yokohama, Rome or Santa Barbara) they asked her to talk about her trip instead of reading a novel. I am sure they would rather hear about the people and the customs of those countries, but my mother, being a mother, told about what was closest to her heart, her children and grandchildren. So that's how they knew.

Some years later, when I was back in my hometown in Sweden, it occurred to me to call "the blind ladies." I was told that the last of them had died the year before.

I found where she was buried and put a red rose on her grave.

21
Travels with Mike

My son Mike was twelve, when George and I divorced. I decided to take him with me on a trip to Europe to see friends and relatives. Before we left, I told Mike, "I think you ought to cut your hair, before we go to Europe."

This was during the hippie era, and my son was in style with shoulder length blond hair—quite pretty, actually.

"Why?" he answered, totally perplexed.

"Well, in Europe boys don't wear long hair. They will think you're a girl."

"Silly Europeans," was his answer.

I didn't want to make an issue of it, so we left for Europe with his long hair intact. Our first stop was Paris, where we stayed with my good friend, Marguerite. The concierge, an elderly woman, whom I knew from previous visits, greeted us with a friendly "*Bonjour Madame, Bonjour, Mademoiselle.*" Mike looked at me, but said nothing.

Our next stop was Madrid. Here, too, we were fortunate to be staying with friends, Julia de la Cuadra, who lived with her elderly mother. They had a couple of servants, which was quite common in Europe at the time. One young girl, not much older than Mike, was assigned to him. She made his bed, washed his clothes, put them away and polished his shoes. For an American boy, who was constantly nagged at to do these things at home, this was heaven. The fact that the girl was pretty did not hurt either. The girl, I am sure, knew he was a boy, but not so Julia's elderly mother, at least not at first. She greeted him with, "*Buenos días, Señorita!*"

"What is it with these old European women?" said Mike in disgust. "Haven't they seen an American boy before?"

"Not with long hair," I said, smiling that I had proven my point

After Spain we went to my sister's log cabin in northern Sweden. No servants here, for sure, and no other luxuries either. Being the only young man around, Mike was put to work. He chopped wood for the fireplace and drew water from the well. These were chores that my California-bred son had never done before, and he did them with little enthusiasm.

One thing he liked though was going fishing with my brother-in-law. That pleasure lost some of its luster, however, when my sister greeted the proud fisherman with, "Cleaning fish is fun, Mike," and put him to work.

My brother invited us to go to Finland, so we took the boat from Stockholm to Helsinki. The trip is lovely, through an archipelago with thousands of islands, some inhabited, some not. But Mike was more interested in the slot machines on board. My brother felt he should lecture his nephew on the evils of gambling, and how he could easily lose all his money. After Mike won the jackpot, my brother stopped lecturing.

In Helsinki my uncle took us to his club for lunch. He spoke no English, so the conversation was in Swedish. Mike did not understand Swedish, and he became bored. When he asked me for some Finnish coins to go to play the slot machine, I gave him some without thinking and continued talking with my uncle.

After a while Mike came back with a puzzled expression on his face.

"What is it, Mike?" I asked.

"Well, I put a Finnish mark in the slot machine, but no money came out, only this," and he showed me a little round, rubbery circle, wrapped in foil. "I don't even know what it is."

But *I* did, and, evidently, so did my uncle and all of the rest of the club members, because they burst out laughing. Mike looked puzzled and a little embarrassed, and since I did not think this was the time and place for a detailed explanation of contraceptives, I just took the item and put it in my purse, saying, "Oh, it's just some silly Finnish souvenir."

Mike forgot all about it, and so did I, until weeks later, when we arrived at customs in the L.A. airport. I suddenly remembered the Finnish "souvenir," which until then, I had completely forgotten. Would they find it? They did. They looked at it, smiled, put it back in my purse, and then looked at me.

They must have been wondering what a middle age woman with a twelve-year old son was doing with a condom in her purse.

When asked about his trip, Mike answered, "Well, the Europeans sure are different. In some countries they can't tell a boy from a girl and the servants do everything for you. In others, *you* have to do everything for *them*. Plus they have the weirdest slot machines."

22

The Countess and the Cockney

Traveling with Mike all over Europe had been a lot of fun and I would had loved to do it again. But the following summer he went to Japan with his father; I went alone to Spain to visit my friends, the Carreños, and then to Nice. I had not reserved a hotel room there, because I planned to stay with friends. But unfortunately something came up, and they couldn't receive me. I went anyway.

When I asked the flight attendant on the flight from Madrid, where she thought I might find a room for the night, she said,

"Oh, Madame, I am afraid that will be impossible. Every room in town has been reserved for weeks because of the trade fair."

"I didn't know about the fair. What am I going to do?" She just shrugged her shoulders and walked away.

"Maybe I can help," said the gentleman sitting next to me. He was good-looking, tall with broad shoulders and spoke with a very clipped British accent.

Well, I wonder what he has in mind, but it won't hurt to hear what he has to say, I thought. He introduced himself as Richard Robertson-Jones from London.

"I always stay at the Negresco, when I am in Nice on business," he said. "They know all the other hotels in town, and they have a much better chance of locating one with a vacancy, than you would on your own."

When he noticed my skeptical look, he smiled and said," Don't worry, I am not going to stay in Nice, but I'll call the Negresco from the airport for you."

Then he looked at me, cleared his throat, and asked, "Do you have any other clothes in your luggage? And also, could you do something about your hair?"

Since I was dressed in jeans, a T-shirt and sandals and had been swimming in the Mediterranean that morning, I understood his critical look. At the same time I wondered, what business that was of his.

"Of course I have other clothes, but the Hotel Negresco is definitely out of my league."

"Yes, I understand, but I have another idea. When we arrive in Nice, I'll call the Negresco and say, 'My *dear friend*, Madame la Comtesse Shirokow, has made a reservation, and I hope that you will do your best to make her feel comfortable.' Since I am a frequent guest, I'm sure they will go out of their way for a *friend* of mine. In the meantime you should get dressed up: high heels, gloves, do something about your hair and take a taxi to the Negresco. There you should *sweep* into the lobby, go directly to the concierge and tell him in your best French, that you hope your "rooms" are ready. It's very important that you say, "my rooms," in the plural."

The whole idea sounded like fun, and what did I have to lose? Mr. Robinson-Jones was right. The Negresco was in a much better position to find a room for me, than I was on my own.

So I did exactly as he suggested. I changed my clothes at the airport, put my hair up in a French twist, took a taxi to the Negresco and *made an entrance.* When I asked the concierge, "Are my rooms ready?" there ensued a great confusion at his desk, since they had never heard of me before Mr. Robertson-Jones's phone call.

Would I please forgive them; there must have been a mistake, the hotel was completely booked; but if Madame la Comtesse would be good enough to wait just a little while, they would do their very best to find her as good a room as possible. They were very sorry, but they might not be able to find a suite on such a short notice, but if Madame la Comtesse would make herself comfortable on the sofa, and accept a glass of champagne, *compliments de l'hôtel,* they would do their utmost to find an accommodation.

I settled down against the pillows, sipped my champagne, and tried to look as much like a countess as I could. I was vaguely aware of a gentleman sitting in a sofa opposite me, looking at me rather quizzically, while drinking a beer, but I was more interested in listening to the concierge's telephone calls. He called for quite a while, one hotel after another.

Finally after about forty-five minutes he found a room in, what I gathered, was a third class hotel. With many apologies, he wondered if I would accept it. I did, with what I hoped sounded like a resigned sigh, got into a taxi (also compliments of the hotel), and left very happy for a small modest hotel nearby.

After a lovely bath where I sent a grateful thought to Mr. Robertson-Jones, I went to have dinner at a little sidewalk restaurant outside the hotel. At the next table sat a gentleman, who looked vaguely familiar. He smiled a little and said with an unmistakable cockney accent, "My compliments, Madame la Comtesse, for a truly great performance at the Negresco."

"How did you know?"

"Your obvious relief, when you got a third class hotel room."

23

Alburria

Meeting people like Mr. Robertson-Jones is one of the fun things about traveling. So is talking to friends about your trips, when you get back. Listening to *their* trips is the price you have to pay.

I thought about that when I asked my friends the Andersons, "In your many travels all over the world did you ever visit a charming little country called Alburria?"

The Andersons travel a great deal. They also like to talk about their travels and show their photos and videos. So do I. The trouble is, I hardly ever get a chance to do so. Whenever I mention what to me is an exotic and unusual place, and the things I have seen and done there, they interrupt with, "Yes, we totally agree with you. Did you go to? Did you see? Did you meet the President?" And it seems that, where *they went*, what *they* saw and what *they* did, was always more interesting, than what I had seen or done. This was getting exceedingly annoying, so when I heard about Alburria, I decided to have some fun with them.

Alburria is a country invented by a dear Russian friend of mine, Vova. Some years ago, when sailing on his yacht in the Adriatic and Aegean seas, he had a crew consisting mostly of Albanians and Bulgarians. It seems he had difficulty telling them apart, so he called them all Alburrians. That was the origin of a fictitious country he called Alburria. Over many a delightful dinner Vova and his friends created the *Communist Republic of Alburria*. The Communist system was one Vova knew well, being a former citizen of the Soviet Union. Its capital became Alburgorod, and its language a Slavic one, similar to Russian. The country's main export was garlic, Vova's favorite spice. And the garlic clove became its symbol. The flag was a garlic clove on red background.

Vova even made up passports for his friends and little flags for their cars, like those that diplomats have, as well as maps showing clearly, where Alburria is located right at the tip of the Horn of Africa.

One of his friends later moved to Washington D.C., where the Alburrian flag on his car became very useful. The traffic cops thought he was a diplomat and thus he could park anywhere he wanted to without getting a ticket. The flag probably would have worked for speeding and DUI as well.

For the passport to look legitimate it had to have some different countries' stamps on it. The first one was the most difficult. Once *one* country had accepted it as legitimate and stamped it, others would follow.

Vova thought long and hard, about which country would be the easiest to fool. He decided on Italy and got his passport stamped in a little town on the French-Italian border.

Over the years he collected quite a few more, although he was not always successful. He had, of course, his American passport in reserve.

So, when I asked my friends, the Andersons, if they had been to *Alburria*, I was curious to hear their answer. They did not disappoint me.

"Yes, we were there, but it was a long time ago and we didn't stay long! We did meet the President and his wife, though. They were charming, but unfortunately they didn't speak English."

24

Toilets of the World

Museums, churches, temples, palaces and castles—you visit these around the world. You love them or you dislike them, you compare them, but above all you mention them, to show off to your friends that you have been there, done that.

But there is another place that you visit wherever you go, because you need to, a place you rarely mention, because it is not considered to be in good taste: the toilet.

In Spain years ago, I encountered one in a private home, which was a combination toilet and shower: two small platforms for your feet, nowhere to sit, and two knobs, one to flush and one for the shower.

Some public toilets in Paris are super-elegant and efficient. In the winter the seats are heated. As you sit down, music plays—classical, naturally. There is only one drawback. The door opens automatically after five minutes. I sometimes needed more time!

I feel a little nostalgic for the old-time Parisian *pissoirs,* as they are called. Even though they are for men only, there was something truly special to, as you pass them, be greeted by a man, lifting his hat to you as you walked by, using his left hand, of course.

Going to a public bathroom in Italy can be confusing, if you don't speak or read the language. One door is marked," Signore," the other "Signori." Since I didn't know which was which, I waited until someone came out. When I saw a Japanese woman come out, I went in there. Trouble was, she didn't read Italian either!

One type of toilet, which chocked even me, is the one on Chinese trains with free water flowing through the coaches, described in Chapter 35.

The most picturesque toilets are the outhouses in the Swedish countryside. There you may sit with the door open, looking at beautiful dark-green pines and yellow wheat fields, listening to the birds singing, and smelling the perfume of lovely wild flowers. Sometimes you may see a deer walk by. If you are shy, you close the door and study the magazine pictures of Swedish kings and queens, which almost always decorate the interior of Swedish out-houses.

In America there are toilets, which flush automatically, when you get up. I find that somewhat disconcerting. What if you change your mind?

I have heard, but I cannot vouch for it, that on the latest super-modern air-planes, there are now separate facilities for men and women. In the women's they supposedly have an automatic tampon remover. I pity the poor man who goes in there by mistake!

25

Taking a Chance on Nobel

As much as I wanted to explore toilets (and other national treasures!) in countries, where I had never been, I also wanted to go back to Sweden, especially after my divorce. I tried to do so at least once a year. All my relatives knew of my visits, so when my sister-in-law in Stockholm called out to my brother, "Axel, come here and look! Your sister is on T.V.," it could very well have been true.

On December 10, 1978, my brother and sister-in-law, like about ninety-nine percent of the Swedes, were watching the King of Sweden give the coveted Nobel Prizes to the laureates from all over the world in the Stockholm Concert Hall.

The founder of the Nobel Prize, Alfred Nobel, is no doubt one of the best-known Swedes in the world. He invented dynamite and, since he was a peace-loving man, we are told that he wanted it used to make tunnels through mountains between countries, so that people would get to know their neighbors. He thought that knowing each other would stop them from fighting each other!

When he died on December 10, 1896, Sweden and Norway were united. The Swedes called it a union, but the Norwegians thought of it as an occupation. Nobel was against the union and showed his feelings by having the peace prize awarded in Oslo, Norway, by the Norwegian Parliament, whereas the other four prizes (now five) are awarded in Stockholm by the King of Sweden.

So, when my brother answered, "Don't be silly, Kerstin is in Santa Barbara. How could she be on Swedish T.V.?" he was wrong.

I was there all right, sitting in one of the front rows with a perfect view of the stage. There they were, all the laureates, receiving their prizes in Medicine, Literature, Physics, Chemistry and Economics. They were dressed in tails and white ties, sitting on one side of the stage and the King and Queen and other members of the royal family, as well as Nobel Committee officials, on the other.

But what in the world was *I* doing there?

On My Way to the Nobel Celebration

This is how that happened. My friend Tom was going to Stockholm on business and wanted me to go with him. We were going on the QE2 and would only be there two days, from the ninth to the eleventh of December, and then continue to Amsterdam. When Tom realized, that we would be in Stockholm during the Nobel festivities, he asked if there was any chance I could get tickets to some of the ceremonies.

I called the Nobel Committee, where I had a friend since my university days. He told me that all tickets were long gone, but that if there were any cancellations, he would keep us in mind.

We checked in at the Grand Hotel just opposite the Royal Palace in Stockholm the day before the big event. It is an old-fashioned *grand* hotel, where most of the laureates stay.

I had not told my brothers and sister that I would be there. I come from a very conservative family, and my siblings would have considered it highly inappropriate for me to spend the night with a gentleman friend.

When we arrived at the hotel, there was a message from the Nobel Committee. The Ambassador from Tanzania and his wife had suddenly taken ill. Would we like to have their tickets? Would we!

The dress code was white tie. That pleased Tom very much. He was a knight of the Order of Malta and, with white tie, he could wear his Cross of Malta, of which he was rightly proud. I must say he looked splendid with the silk sash and the White Cross.

While we were dressing, the phone rang. There had been two cancellations for the big dinner and ball at the Town Hall, following the ceremony. Would we be interested in those tickets? You bet!

Off we went to the ceremony at the Concert Hall. Since we had the tickets of the Ambassador of Tanzania, we were seated in one of the front rows, reserved for African diplomats. Our entrance caused a bit of a stir. The African diplomats obviously knew one another. Who were we? Besides, we really stood out—two pale faces in a row of black ones. There were a lot of turned heads and whispering. After a few minutes the King came in dressed in his royal uniform with the wide blue sash across his chest. King Carl XVI Gustav is good-looking, and twenty-seven years ago he looked even better.

When the orchestra played the National Anthem, I was the first one in our row to stand up, and the only one who knew the words. The T.V. cameras picked it all up, and that's how my incognito trip to Stockholm was broadcast on Swedish National T.V. But that was not the end of it.

At the ball afterwards we were given the seats of two journalists who hadn't been able to come. There were place cards and mine read, "Anna Larsson." The gentleman sitting next to me looked at me in a puzzled way and finally said, "Excuse me. I know Anna Larsson and you are not Anna Larsson."

I explained the whole story and he thought it very amusing; so amusing, in fact, that he wrote an article about it in Stockholm's leading newspaper, where he was a journalist. He called the article *Taking a Chance on Nobel.*

In it he described how two Americans, Kerstin Shirokow and Tom Johnson, had come all the way from Santa Barbara, CA., and managed to participate in the Nobel festivities by sheer luck.

So my sister, who for some reason had missed me on television, read all about it in the morning paper!

So much for incognito.

26

The Kings and I

Speaking English, French and Spanish had certainly been useful traveling the world, but who would have thought that *Swedish* might be? I mean, who wants to learn Swedish? A totally useless language I always thought, except for the nine million Swedes. And yet, it was because of knowing Swedish that I could go to America, first to Augustana College, and then to the Language School, where I met my husband. And now, thanks to Swedish, I was about to have a truly glamorous experience.

"Oh, you are Swedish! Great! Then you can tell me what to say to the King of Sweden, who will be visiting San Francisco next week. I am the official greeter in the mayor's absence."

Cyril Magnin, related to I. Magnin and also a business tycoon, greeted me warmly at a cocktail party, to which a friend had brought me.

"I sure can, Mr. Magnin," I said. "You say '*Välkommen till San Francisco, Ers Majestät.*'"

"Oh, dear," he said, "that's difficult. Could you possibly come up to my office tomorrow and record it on tape, so I can practice? I'd be extremely grateful."

"I'd be glad to," I answered.

Cyril Magnin was a nice old gentleman and if I could help him and at the same time do my bit to further Swedish-American relations, why not?

The next day I went to his office and recorded the greeting. Mr. Magnin listened and repeated it a few times. I corrected him, and then left, suggesting he repeat it a few times a day until the arrival of the king.

With the King and Queen of Sweden

The day for the king's visit arrived, and the Swedish American Chamber of Commerce had a reception for him. To my great surprise I was invited, too. Cyril Magnin was there and, when the king arrived, he went up to him and said in perfect Swedish, "*Välkommen till San Francisco, Ers Majestät.*"

The king was very surprised and said, "Well, thank you, Mr. Magnin. I am amazed and flattered, that you can say that in Swedish. Where did you learn to say that?"

"She taught me," said Mr. Magnin and pointed to me. The king turned around, saw me and waved to me to come forward. I did, and we chatted for a few minutes.

There was a photographer present, so my mother had something to show her friends in Sweden.

◆   ◆   ◆

This was not the only time, however, that I met a King of Sweden. The present king's grandfather, King Gustav VI Adolf was a respected archeologist, who frequently visited Cerveteri, the old Etruscan gravesite outside of Rome.

During one of his visits in the sixties, when I lived in Rome with my family, I took my children to St. Peter's Cathedral. I first showed them the great tomb of Queen Kristina of Sweden and told them, "This Queen is the only woman buried in the cathedral. The Pope wanted to show his respect for the queen of a protestant country, who abdicated her throne to convert to Catholicism. This happened in 1654."

"And you're named after her, right?" said my son.

"Well, not exactly, but Kerstin is an abbreviation of Kristina."

While I was explaining all that to my children, a voice behind me said, in Swedish, "You seem to know the history of my country as well as I do."

I turned around, and there was King Gustav VI Adolf of Sweden, about to explain to his granddaughter, Princess Christina, pretty much what I had just told my children.

This was my week of royal encounters. A couple of days later, as I was attending classes in Italian at *Scuola Dante Alghieri*, (named after the poet *Dante*, who wrote *Divina Commedia*), the professor said we could take a break to witness the arrival of the King of Sweden. The main archeological office was in the school.

We students went out into the yard and, after a few minutes, the king arrived in a big black limousine with Swedish flags in front. He stepped out and for some reason there was no one there to meet him. The poor king stood there with his chauffeur, looking a little lost, so I called out in Swedish: "Welcome to our school, Your Majesty!"

He turned around, smiled and said, also in Swedish, "Thank you very much."

At that moment an official from the archeological department arrived, just when the King and I were becoming acquainted!

27

Cops, Cars, and Bikinis

In the 1980's I found another use for my native tongue. I was hired by the University of California in Santa Barbara to teach Swedish. Who would ever have thought Swedish would be taught at U.C.S.B? I certainly didn't. But there was indeed a Swedish program, part of the larger Germanic Languages Division. The Swedish professor was a friend of mine; and, when she became pregnant, she suggested me as a replacement for a year.

Although I didn't have a doctoral degree, I was hired; the fact that I was dating the head of the Germanic Languages Department probably didn't hurt either.

To celebrate my being hired, my friend Tom threw a party for me at his house. Much champagne was consumed by everybody and especially by me!

While driving home at one-thirty in the morning after the celebration in my honor, I was feeling great—until I saw the red flashing lights behind me and heard, "Please pull off to the side!"

After I did, the officer said, "Please show me your driver's license and registration. Do you know that you were driving too fast and weaving from side to side??

"Well, let me explain, Officer," I said. "You see, I have just been hired to teach at UCSB, and I am sure you understand that I had to celebrate that!"

He was not the least bit impressed. Instead he asked me, "Please get out of the car, put your hands behind your back, look up at the stars and walk a straight line."

I couldn't do it, of course, and when I asked him, "Officer, would *you* be able to do it in high heels?" he was not amused.

Then he asked me, "Please recite the alphabet." I did, in Swedish. He said he didn't understand a single sound, so I said, "But, Officer, you didn't specify which language. Do you want to hear it French?"

"Ma'am, this is no joke," he answered

All of a sudden I realized the seriousness of my situation, and sobered up quickly. "Officer," I said. "I am glad you stopped me. I could have caused a terrible accident. I don't feel very well. If you could drive ahead of me until I get home, I would be ever so grateful. Could you, please?"

He thought about it for a moment, and then he said, "O.K." And so he did. When we came to my house in Montecito, he drove through the gates all the way up to the front door. I went out to thank him and said, "Officer, you have been so kind and nice. Would you like to come in for a beer?"

"Don't push it, lady," he said and drove off.

He was one nice cop, and there have been others.

◆   ◆   ◆

In Italy, my husband and I were driving on Via Appia outside of Rome, when two *carabinieri* (traffic police) stopped us. We were driving our new 1964 Mercedes sport convertible, which we had picked up the week before at the factory in Germany. The car was black with red leather upholstery, and a beauty. Since the model was not yet being sold in Italy, wherever we went people stopped to admire it. So did the two *carabinieri,* who had just stopped us. (There are always *two*; they say one knows how to read, the other how to write!)

"You speak to them in your best Italian," my husband quickly said, "and unbutton your blouse a little bit more."

I followed his advice, just as they rode up.

"*Scusi, Signora,*" one of them said, "we are sorry, but you were driving too fast, so we must give you a ticket."

"I know, officer," I answered in Italian, "but you see, we couldn't help it. This brand new car, it goes so fast, we can't seem to slow it down."

"Well, if that is the case," he answered, "you should drive it on the Autostrada, not on a 2000-year old road."

"Well, yes," I answered, "but on the Autostrada we would not meet handsome *carabinieri* like you." I gave them an appreciative look and a big smile.

"*Madonna mia,*" he said, and waved us on.

Another time, when I was approached by cops, I wasn't even in a car. I was at a swimming pool in Madrid, when two *guardas civiles* (policemen) came up to me. I was wearing a bikini, which was strictly forbidden in Franco's puritanical Spain in the late forties. I knew that, but some Spanish friends encouraged me to wear it to see what would happen.

They were watching intently, when the *guardas* came up to me and said, "*Señorita,* we realize you are a foreigner and don't know the rules, but we don't permit bathing suits in two pieces here."

"*Muy bien,*" I answered, "which piece would you like me to take off?"

28

On The Fence

"Thank God, you are here, Mr. Takahashi. The Japanese Consul General has been waiting for over half an hour," I said, as I led our friend, Taro Takahashi, into our living room.

"Wait, I have to go on the toilet first," he answered.

I showed him to the bathroom.

"By the way, the Americans say, 'I want to wash my hands,' not 'I want to go on the toilet.'"

He gave me a look of innocent surprise, and said in a puzzled tone of voice, "But I don't want to just wash my hands."

"Never mind, that's what they say," I told him, showed him the bathroom, and then ushered him in to greet the Consul General.

◆   ◆   ◆

I first met Mr. Takahashi in Japan in 1964, the year Tokyo hosted the Olympics. At that time it was quite common for Japanese men to relieve themselves in public against a wall or a fence. Mr. Takahashi realized, that was not the custom in the western world and that it was, in fact, quite offensive to most westerners.

So he tried to do something about it. Since he was involved with the publicity of the Games, he had thousands of posters printed of a man urinating. Underneath was printed in Japanese and in English: "We must stop this for the Olympics."

The posters were distributed in Tokyo and in other major cities in Japan. Whether they caused the Japanese to change their habits is difficult to say, but the signs were an endless cause of amusement among westerners.

Mr. Takahashi frequently asked my advice on American idiomatic expressions, and made me promise always to correct any mistakes he made in English.

About six months later he visited us again. As I met him at the door, I could not resist asking him, "Takahashisan, would you like to wash your hands?"

"No, thank you," he said, "I already washed them on the fence."

29

My Husband's First Wife

She was my husband George's first wife and her name was Natasha. She was also Russian. They met in prison camp in Aschaffenburg, Germany, where they were imprisoned after the German offensive against the Soviet Union in 1942.

The camp was a tough labor camp, where the Germans put the non-Aryan prisoners, like the Russians, Poles and other Slavs. Whereas the Jews had to wear the Star of David on their sleeves, the Russians had to wear a large "O" for *Osten*, e.g. Easterner.

George's and Natasha's was not a romantic love story. Rather they sought comfort in each other. When Natasha became pregnant, there was no way to get a safe abortion, so they married and had the child.

They divorced when the war was over, and Natasha managed to immigrate to the U.S. first. She found a job teaching Russian at the Army Language School in Monterey, California. When George eventually came to the U.S., she helped him get a position at the same school.

They had now left the horrors of war behind, and had started a new life in a free country. They had a son together, Alexander, so decided to live together, and give marriage another try.

It didn't work. George didn't love her; never really had, although Natasha loved him. So he moved out, and rented a room from a Russian colleague. That's where he lived, when I was hired to teach Swedish at the school. By that time Natasha wasn't teaching there anymore.

George and I met, fell in love and married. After we returned from our honeymoon, odd things began to happen. The phone would ring, but when I answered, there was nobody there, just somebody breathing. There were threatening, unsigned notes in my mailbox, sometimes in my car. I didn't know from whom they came, but I had my suspicions.

Natasha wouldn't let George visit their son, which hurt George very much. My father-in-law was allowed to see the child, and he would tell George about Alexander, but it wasn't the same as seeing him.

One day, a Russian friend of ours, who also knew Natasha, thought it would be *fun,* if the two Mrs. Shirokows met. So she invited us to a cocktail party and introduced us to each other.

"You two should get to know each other," she said. You have a lot in common," and she laughed.

It was an unpleasant experience for me and must have been very painful and embarrassing for Natasha. She was beautiful, with dark hair and black eyes, and she played the piano equal to a concert pianist. I was her complete contrast, blond and blue-eyed, with no particular talents. I felt rather colorless and insignificant by comparison. But the biggest difference was on the inside; in how our different lives and experiences had shaped our characters and personalities.

Natasha had seen mankind at its worst. She had been starved and tortured. To get food for her child she had been forced to humiliate herself with German soldiers. She trusted nobody.

I, on the other hand, grew up in a small town in neutral Sweden. I was totally secure in every way amid a large, loving family, in a town where everybody knew everybody else. To me the world was a wonderful place, and I believed in the goodness of people.

George later told me that this was one of the things he loved about me.

◆   ◆   ◆

I didn't see Natasha for forty years, until one day when I was at the hospital, where her son, my stepson, was dying of leukemia. Outside the door I saw an old lady, who looked at me in a strange way. She said in a heavy Russian accent: "You must be Kerstin."

I looked at her. Did I know her? How did she know my name?

"Natasha?" I asked.

"Yes," she replied.

We hugged each other and cried.

We were mothers now, not wives of the same husband.

30

Black Viking

"What does one have to do to get a drink around here?" I said out loud to nobody in particular. Everybody else seemed to have a drink in hand at this beautiful cocktail party in the garden of an elegant Montecito estate.

The party was in honor of a writer, a friend of the hostess's. Most of the guests, I gathered, were from Barnaby and Mary Conrad's Santa Barbara Writer's Conference. My escort had attended the conference and had invited me to come with him.

William Buckley, Jr. had been entertaining us with some of his sailing adventures, and not far away was the well-known local writer Fanny Flagg, telling an amusing anecdote. Unfortunately, I couldn't really enjoy either one, because I wanted a drink! An eternity ago, it seemed, I had asked Dick, my escort, to get one, but he seemed to have disappeared forever.

I didn't really want to leave the interesting conversations that were going on around me, but finally my thirst got the better of me and I set out on a quest for a bar. Eventually I found one, well stocked from the looks of it, but wouldn't you know it, no bartender in sight!

Looking around I saw a black man in tuxedo standing not too far away. Good, I thought, I found the bartender. I went up to him an d said, "Why aren't you behind the bar?"

He looked a little surprised, but went immediately behind the bar and asked, "What would you like, Ma'm?'

"I would like a vodka gimlet, not on the rocks but well chilled."

"Certainly, Ma'm," he said, and fixed me best vodka gimlet I have ever had. Boy, did it taste good! Just the right amount of Rose's sweetened lime juice and straight up, not on the rocks, yet still perfectly chilled. This bartender could surely fix a drink!

Thus fortified, I joined the others and listened with great pleasure to Ray Bradbury telling about his new science fiction story, and Charles Schultz regaling us with Snoopy's latest escapades.

All of a sudden the hostess clapped her hands and asked us to join her in welcoming the guest of honor. As we slowly gathered around, I saw to my utter horror, that the guest of honor was the black man in the tuxedo, whom I had mistaken for the bartender and asked to fix me a drink! Talk about embarrassment! That's not the word for it. There exists no word for what I felt. I wanted to run away, disappear from the surface of the earth, and die on the spot! But of course I couldn't do any of those things. I had to go up to him and say "hello." What I said or rather stuttered or blabbered, I don't remember, but he, a perfect gentleman, brushed away all my apologies and asked me instead, what I thought of his book *Black Viking*. He wanted *my* opinion of his book, after the way I had behaved!

I told him that, although I had Viking blood in my veins, I never knew there had been any *black* Vikings. He explained how documents show that the Vikings went as far south as Morocco, so consequently it is quite possible that they fathered children there.

When I asked him if, in spite of my boorish behavior, he would sign his book for me, he smiled and wrote: "Dear Kerstin, just think, maybe one day all bartenders will be Swedish."

Bill Downey taught me a lesson that day I'll never forget. May he rest in peace.

31

The Gift of the Mafia

"Remember, Cristina, when you get to Sicily, there is one word you mustn't mention. Ever! That's *mafia*," said my friend, Anna Maria. My other Roman friends agreed.

"Come on, Anna Maria. I may be Swedish, but I do know that much," I answered.

"Why are you going to Sicily anyway?" asked Paolo. "Stay here in Rome with us. There is nothing for you in *Sicilia*, the people there are '*sin cultura*' (uncultured) and most of them are *Mafiosi."* Many Romans look down upon other Italians, especially those living south of Rome, such as Calabrians and Sicilians.

"*Sono tutti Saraceni,* "(They are all Saracens), said Paolo, referring to tribes of nomad Arabs, who harassed the frontiers of the Roman Empire 1500 years ago. Not to be undone, the non-Romans got back with their interpretation of the letters S.P.Q.R. (*Senatus Popolusque Romanus*), Latin for "the Senate and the Roman people," with which all the manhole covers in Rome are inscribed. The non-Romans say it stands for "*Sono Porchi Questi Romani*" (These Romans are pigs).

So why was I going to Sicily? I was beginning to wonder myself. A couple of months earlier at the Coral Casino, a swim club in Santa Barbara, the mayor of Santa Barbara, who was a friend of mine and, like me, an avid swimmer, asked me one day, "You speak Italian, Kerstin, don't you?"

"Yes, I do," I answered. "I lived in Italy for three years in the sixties, and I often go back to visit friends."

"Good," he said. "Will you come to my office to translate a letter I just received from the mayor of Paterno?"

Paterno is a small town at the foot of the volcano Etna in Sicily. I was surprised and curious, because it is practically unknown outside of Sicily. Why would its mayor write to the mayor of Santa Barbara? I soon found out.

"My name is Salvatore Sinatra," the letter began. *"I am the mayor of Paterno. I and the people of my town would very much like our town to become a sister city of Santa Barbara. Paterno has two sister cities in Europe but none in the New World. Although I have never been to the United States, I have heard that Santa Barbara is by the ocean and grows oranges, just like Paterno, and therefore I think would be a perfect choice for a sister city.*
Warm greetings, and I am looking forward to hearing from you!"
Salvatore Sinatra.

At that time Santa Barbara already had three sister cities: Puerto Vallarta in Mexico, Toba in Japan and Cuzco in Peru. The mayor thought it a good idea to have one in Italy, too. He suggested that, since I was going to Italy anyway, I take a letter from him to Signor Sinatra, agreeing with the proposal. A date was agreed upon to meet in Catania, the Cicilian port city closest to the Italian mainland.

When I disembarked from the ferryboat in Catania, the first thing I saw was a sign," *Benvenuta, Cristina di Santa Barbara!*" Two men who could have been extras in the movie *The Godfather* held the banner! One, the mayor's deputy no doubt, even had a bulge under his left arm. The other man, I discovered, was the mayor himself, Salvatore Sinatra.

In a chauffeur-driven limousine I was escorted to the mayor's house, where I met his wife, Lucia, their son, Pasquale, and their German shepherd, Adolf. A week of festivities followed. I was the honored guest of the *Onorevole sindaco* (honored mayor) Salvatore Sinatra, and of the whole town of Paterno. There were excursions to the top of the volcano, Mount Etna, which is still active, and to the ancient Greek theater of Taormina. I visited schools and talked to school-children. The culmination was a beach party for about thirty people, where speeches were given and toasts exchanged. It ended with, *"Viva Santa Barbara, viva Cristina e viva Presidente Carter!"*

Then I had to make a speech, in Italian naturally, which I spoke but not perfectly. I thanked them for the wonderful welcome I had been given, and ended with a phrase borrowed from President Kennedy's speech to the people of Berlin: *"Ich bin ein Berliner* (I am a Berliner)." But I said, *"Io sono Paternese* (I am Paternese)." That, they liked!

On the day of my departure the mayor called me to his office for a ceremony of exchanging gifts. Salvatore Sinatra said he wanted to give to Santa Barbara a sample of Sicily's biggest export to the United States. Then he took from behind his back a little statue of a Mafioso, a tough-looking guy with his hat down over one eye and a bulge under his left arm, where he kept his gun. So much for my friends' warnings!

Shortly after my return to Santa Barbara a group of about thirty people from Paterno came to visit. The mayor and I met them at the airport with a sign, "*Benvenuti a Santa Barbara!*" Then we took them to the Best Western motel. We had previously arranged for them to stay with various Italian-speaking families, but not one of our guests spoke a word of English and, we learned later that most of them had never been out of Sicily! They wanted to stay together, and had heard of Best Western, so that's where we made reservations.

The first evening we had a big party at my house, organized with the help of the Sons of Italy and the Boot Club. We provided music and dancing, and I had the unique experience of dancing a tarantella with *il onorevole Salvatore Sinatra!*

Among them was a local Paterno painter, who brought with him fifteen of his oil paintings to be displayed, he hoped, at the Santa Barbara Museum of Art. When told that couldn't be arranged, he was very disappointed. So we decided to put them up in my office, and some locals of Italian descent were gently persuaded to buy some. I believe three were bought. The painter gave me one of a donkey pulling a load of hay, which still hangs in my kitchen.

The sister city relationship between our two cities became a very fruitful one. School children from Paterno wrote to our school children and vice versa. Many Santa Barbara visitors were warmly welcomed in Paterno over the years. When an American warship anchored off the coast of Cantania, not far from Paterno, their people were invited on board. Later on, Paterno arranged for a soccer match between the ship's sailors and a local team.

The statuette of the Mafioso, Paterno's gift to Santa Barbara, stood for many years in a display case in City Hall. When I contacted the mayor's office to take a picture of it recently, I was told it was no longer there. I called a few of the previous mayors personally, but nobody knew where Santa Barbara's Mafioso had ended up.

The sister city relationship ended about three years ago by mutual consent.

The statuette of the Mafioso was never found.

32

My Olympic Team

My Olympic Team

During the Olympic games in Los Angeles in 1984 I served as an aide to the canoeing-kayaking team, which represented The Ivory Coast in West Africa. I became their aide purely by chance.

The rowing and other boating competitions were held at Lake Casitas and Lake Cachuma, near Santa Barbara. Competing athletes from all over the world lived in dormitories on the U.C.S.B. campus. Among them was the Swedish women's rowing team. I wanted to be involved in the games, so I applied for a position as an aide-interpreter for that team. Unfortunately, that position was already taken, but since I speak French, I was asked, if I wanted to become an aide to the French-speaking team from the Ivory Coast. I accepted, and the following two weeks became some of the most interesting I have ever spent.

The team consisted of four athletes, one coach and one doctor of sports medicine. I helped them, not only with the language, (none of them spoke a word of English) but also with any problem that might come up. The athletes were around twenty years old, tall and slim, with not an ounce of fat, broad shoulders, narrow hips and very, very black. They had never been outside their respective villages; each one of them spoke a different language. The only language they had in common was French, which the French government had made mandatory while the country was under French rule. When The Ivory Coast became independent in 1960, French remained its national language.

To these young men everything in the U.S. was strange and new: coin-operated telephones, for example. I helped one of them make a call to his mother in Abidjan. Figuring it would cost about forty dollars, I went to a bank to get one hundred and sixty quarters, and stood by him plunking in the quarters while he was talking to his mother.

One day I received a telephone call from the mother of a young lady who without my knowledge had befriended Antoine, one of the team members. There was a serious misunderstanding, and I was asked to come and help, since neither she nor her daughter, Lisa, spoke French. I found a very annoyed mother, a bewildered Lisa and a totally miserable Antoine. He cried and said he couldn't understand why Lisa didn't want to kiss him anymore and didn't even want to go out with him. How could she say she didn't love him after all the kisses they had shared?

What had happened could best be described as a clash between two cultures. Antoine and Lisa had been dating. Who knows how intimate they had become. Apparently they had at least kissed. To Antoine that was a serious commitment; to Lisa, a typical white American girl, it was nothing but a harmless flirtation. So, when Lisa wanted to break up with Antoine, he was devastated. In his village, when a woman and a man kissed, that meant that they were in love with each other, which in turn almost always lead to marriage. When I explained to them the cultural difference in the meaning of kissing, Lisa said she was sorry, but Antoine was so distraught he stopped training for several days. For an Olympic athlete, that is serious. He eventually began his training again, but the whole incident was obviously a big blow to the team.

The team doctor was an educated man who had received his medical training at the University of Sorbonne in Paris. He was older than the athletes, in his thirties I believe. The doctor was big and fat and often wore a light blue caftan with embroidered borders. He looked magnificent, and raised quite a few eyebrows among the members of the Country Club, where I took him for lunch one day.

After I had learnt, that the three major religions of the Ivory Coast were Catholicism, Islam and Animism, I asked, which he believed in. He said he was an Animist; he worshipped nature.

"So you pray to animals, rocks and trees?" I asked.

"Well, let me tell you more about it, Christine," he said. "You have told me that you love to walk on the beach, to see the sunsets and the sunrises. When you do that and feel the warm sand under your feet and the cool ocean water, don't you sometimes have a grateful feeling in your heart for all the beauty? That is similar to what we animists feel about life around us."

His explanation helped me to better to understand this fascinating nature religion, and it didn't seem so strange anymore.

I wanted to be with my athletes as much as I could. I tried to eat as many meals as possible with them. We had interesting conversations and I learned about the unusual aspects of their culture.

One day when I had breakfast with Antoine, he said, "*tu as l'air si triste, Christine*." (You look so sad).

I told him that my beloved German shepherd, whom I had had for fifteen years, since she was a puppy, had died.

"Oh, I understand perfectly, he said. "Shortly before I left for America, my pet elephant died, and I miss her terribly."

One of the duties of an Olympic aide is to protect the team from the public. Visitors and callers are not allowed to contact them without first checking with the aide, in order to help the athletes concentrate on their sports.

One day I received a phone call from a Los Angeles representative of the NAACP. She wanted to speak to the members of my team and was very annoyed, that she had to go through me.

"You are certainly welcome to talk to the athletes," I said, "but you realize I have to be present."

"No, I don't realize that at all," she answered. "I want to talk to them freely, and I believe I can do it better without you."

"Well, I don't know about that," I said. "You do speak French of course? They don't speak a word of English." She didn't speak French, so agreed to have me present to interpret.

The interview was most interesting. First I had to introduce her. How do you explain to a group of Ivory Coast citizens, what the *National Association for the Advancement of Colored People* is? In their country everybody is black. Nobody is "colored." What "advancement" was she talking about? Compared to whom and over whom? The athletes were totally bewildered and confused. The NAACP lady was visibly upset and wondered if I had translated correctly. Finally she ignored me and tried to speak directly to the athletes in English. They turned to me and asked in French what she was saying. That did not please the NAACP lady!

The two weeks passed far too quickly, and regretfully we had to say "good-bye." My team did not win a medal; as a matter of fact they came in last.

I corresponded with Antoine for a while, and in 1985 I received a photograph of him, his wife and their baby daughter. I was happy to know that he had recovered from his love for Lisa.

33

Proposition in Black and White

Included in Alfonse's letter was an invitation to come and visit them. I was tempted to accept, but didn't want to go alone. I had been told that it wasn't wise for a woman, especially a white woman, to travel alone in Africa. When I asked my son Mike to come with me, he didn't want to leave his girlfriend. So, I asked my daughter Katya. She said, "Mama, I would love to go to Africa, but let's go to Zaïre and see the gorillas."

Gorillas in the "Mint"

We had both just read Diane Fossey's book, *The Gorillas in the Mist,* about her life with the mountain gorillas and we decided to go there instead.

Unbeknownst to us, a civil war had just broken out in Zaïre between two rival tribes, the Hutus and the Tutsis. So our travel agent arranged for a guide to stay with us for safety during the two weeks we were in Africa. That worked out great for us, because now we had the same guide all the time, instead of having a separate one for each stop.

The guide's name was Dave. He was a citizen of Zimbabwe, but his parents were English. He took us to many interesting towns, like Goma and Bujumbura. Once he took us on a boat ride on a river and we jumped in and swam for quite awhile. When we came back to the shore, there was a large crocodile sleeping on the riverbank!

Before we went to see the gorillas, Dave told us, "When you meet the gorillas, you mustn't touch them. But if they want to touch you, you should let them. Try to imitate the sounds they make. It is similar to human burping. Also pretend to eat leaves the way they do."

So we did. As we sat there burping and eating leaves, a baby gorilla jumped from a tree and landed right in my lap! I was delighted to have this adorable baby in my arms, but that was before I saw a huge silverback coming towards us! Maybe it was the father?! I tried to move away, but couldn't without touching the baby. All of a sudden the baby jumped away towards the silverback and they both disappeared in the jungle.

Bon Appétit

The next morning we climbed into a jeep, which would take us up to the gorillas. All of a sudden the jeep stopped. We had come to the end of the road. No more roads: only lava rock, a long walk, and no cabin in sight. My daughter was wearing her hiking boots, but I had foolishly changed to more comfortable shoes for the jeep ride. They were much too thin for lava rock. Fortunately, out of nowhere, about twenty natives appeared, who offered to help carry our luggage.

As I stumbled along, the young man who was carrying my luggage on his head, told me to grab his arm for support, which I gratefully did. He asked why I had so much trouble walking. When I showed him my shoes with the thin soles, my daughter, who walked just ahead of me, turned and said, "Mama, *he* is barefoot!"

After awhile I noticed that my gallant escort seemed to move closer and closer to me. All of a sudden he said, "*Je suis fort, je suis jeune et ma cabine est tout près d'ici.*" (I'm strong, I'm young, and my cabin is very near here)

I was speechless. Here I was, old enough to be his grandmother, being propositioned by an African teenager, while stumbling across lava rock in the middle of Africa! I wondered if my daughter had heard. Her uproarious laughter confirmed she had. My reply required diplomatic consideration. I *needed* the support of my ardent escort, so I replied, "I am flattered and grateful, but my daughter would be very upset, if I left her."

"*Ta fille? Ça, c'est ta fille?*" (Your daughter? That's your daughter?), he said with great surprise, then looked at me, I think, for the first time. But he wasn't easily discouraged.

"Do you have any books I can have? I am practicing reading and really need some."

"I am sorry, I don't have any," I said. "On a trip like this, where you have to carry everything with you, you don't bring any extras."

"What about shoes? As you can see, I don't have any."

I just shook my head.

We finally reached our destination. I said a quick "goodbye" and "thank you," then hurried into the safety of the cabin. Our guide distributed money to all the luggage carriers, including mine.

But passion was apparently in the air, because after dinner, the cabin-keeper, who was also the cook, wanted to share his bed with our handsome guide. My daughter was quite put out. She was the only one, who hadn't been propositioned.

"Wait until tomorrow," I consoled her, "when we meet the gorillas. Maybe some handsome silverback will wink at you!"

34

Her Name Is Kerstin

Not long ago, over fifty years after I arrived in the U.S. to teach at Augustana College, as I was writing in my study in Santa Barbara, I received a phone call. A man's deep, sexy voice said," May I speak to Kerstin Shirokow, please?" He pronounced my first name correctly, *Cheshtin*, as a Swede would, but I could hear he was not a Swede.

"This is Kerstin," I answered.

"This is Ben Fuller," he said. "Remember me?"

"I remember your voice," I said, not quite truthfully. "Give me a hint."

"Augustana College, Rock Island, Illinois 1951."

I tried to think back fifty-six years. (I, who these days, can't remember what I had for dinner yesterday!) and slowly a warm feeling came over me, and I remembered a handsome young man, with whom I shared a lot of fun that long time ago. This was incredible!

"Where are you"? How did you find me? How did you get my number? How did you know my married name?"

"Hold it, hold it!" he said. "I can hear you haven't changed a bit. Calm down, and I'll tell you. I have never forgotten you, nor your Swedish name, Kerstin Hård af Segerstad. I remember you told me it means *Hard of Victory Town*; and, since it is an aristocratic name, nobody but your family has it. So I got on the Internet, found a Peder Hård af Segerstad, and asked him about a Kerstin. He said he knew of one, a distant cousin of his, whose married name is Shirokow, and who he believed lives in Santa Barbara. So I looked up your number and called you, and here I am!"

"But where are you?" I said. "Where are you calling from?"

"I am calling from Edmonton, Alberta."

"But that's in Canada! So far away! Any chance that you will come to Santa Barbara?"

"I don't think so," he said, "my wife doesn't like to travel, and she doesn't want to be too far away from our children and grandchildren."

Wife, children, grandchildren! I don't know why I was so disappointed, but somehow I was.

Quickly I said, "Oh, you have children! Great! How many?"

"I have four children and eight grandchildren. My oldest daughter is named Kerstin."

35

Professor An-Fu and the Tape Recorder

Traveling to far away countries with totally different cultures, like Africa and South America, had really made my travel juice flow. And there was so much more of the world to see. China came to mind. Not even Aunt Elsa had been there!

When I contacted the Chinese Embassy to inquire about a visa, they told me that the easiest way to get it would be to go on a group visa; be a member of a group, which traveled together. That didn't appeal to me at all. Either I'd go with a friend or else alone.

Going alone was not allowed, I was told, unless somebody who lived in China would sponsor me. That meant a person who would guarantee to take care of me, if I were to get sick and be responsible if I committed a crime.

Luckily I had a friend, Marge Hoffman, who worked at the American Embassy in Beijing. I called her and she said, "Of course, I'll sponsor you," and thus I got my visa.

Before leaving, I invited a Chinese friend of mine, Victoria Chuan, to come to my house for dinner with her two teen-aged children.

How Victoria and her children had come to the United States, I didn't know. I *did* know that her hands had been practically ruined during the Cultural Revolution in the seventies. They looked hideous, like the hands of a gorilla without fur. Every day, all day long, she was forced to use her hands for digging and planting without any tools or gloves. At night she practiced playing on a cardboard keyboard, because before the Revolution she had been a concert pianist. After coming to the States her hands recovered somewhat, and she was now teaching piano at City College, where we met.

After dinner I handed her my tape recorder and asked to please record ten useful phrases in preparation for my trip to China.

"You think ten Chinese phrases is all you need to travel alone in China?" she asked, laughing.

"No, but I think that is about all I can learn on the plane over," I answered.

"By the way," she asked, "are you going to Shanghai?"

"I don't know. I want to very much. But it is complicated. A private individual can't book a seat on a plane in advance, so I won't know until the same day, if I'll get a seat or not. Why do you ask?"

"My husband lives there," she said.

"Your husband? Are you divorced?"

"Oh no," she laughed. "Chinese people don't divorce."

She told me that her husband, An-Fu, a professor of Biology, had had his education paid for by the government and was obliged to pay back the debt. This meant that he had to teach in Shanghai until he was sixty-five years old. Only *then* would he be allowed to join his family in California.

"So you can only talk with him on the phone," I said.

"Oh, no," she laughed again. "He has no telephone."

For years neither she nor her children had seen or spoken to their husband and father!

Then I had an idea. Why not ask Victoria and her children to record greetings to professor An-Fu on the other side of the tape? Then, if I had the opportunity to meet him, he would be able to hear their voices for the first time in many years.

They made the recording and then Victoria took a Polaroid picture of me. She put it in an envelope with An-Fu's address written in Chinese and suggested I mail it to him from Beijing, if I found I could indeed go to Shanghai. She explained it was better, if the address were written in Chinese and if the letter were mailed from China. Otherwise it might cause difficulties for An-Fu. She also gave me some pictures of her children to give to their father.

A month later I was on a plane from Beijing to Shanghai. When I landed, I saw a gentleman with my photo on his lapel. I was even wearing the same striped dress! Professor An-Fu had received my letter and was there to meet me. He hailed a taxi, which took me to the hotel, where I asked him to meet me later for dinner.

When he came up to the room, I pretended I wasn't quite ready, so I asked him to wait, while I finished in the bathroom and suggested he listen to a tape while waiting. Then I turned on the recording which Victoria and their children had made, and closed the bathroom door.

After a couple of minutes I came out and saw An-Fu sitting on the bed, tears streaming down his cheeks.

"May I listen to it one more time?" he asked.

"You can have it," I said, "I know the phrases on the other side."

But then it hit me. What good would the tape do him without the tape recorder? Should I give it to him? The tape recorder, which I had brought with me to record the sounds of China! It became a fight between generosity and selfishness, and generosity won. His smile was worth the decision.

.

With Professore An-fu in Shanghai

Professor An-Fu was a perfect guide and showed me many interesting temples and beautiful parks in Shanghai; I saw and visited places I never would have found on my own. From Shanghai I planned to fly to Guilin, where, according to Chinese legend, Paradise is located. I had heard it is full of beautiful lakes and rivers, surrounded by rounded mountaintops, like those you see in Chinese paintings.

When I told professor An-Fu this, he said, "You can't do that. All the flights for the next couple of days are reserved for Communist party officials, who are going to Guilin for a convention. Why don't you take the train?"

"The train?" I asked. "But Guilin is far from Shanghai. I would have to take a sleeping car, and I don't know how to handle that."

"Don't worry," said Professor An-Fu. "I'll go with you, and get you settled." So, with his help, I procured a first class sleeping compartment. I was in luck; there were three beds in the compartment, but I was the only passenger.

The train started moving; I waved goodbye to Professor An-Fu and went to the restaurant car. After a delicious meal, (I had no idea what I ate. To order, I pointed at pictures) I returned to my cabin. Two gentlemen were there. I don't know who were the most surprised, they or I.

Now it was time to go bed. I wondered how I would undress in their presence. I finally took my pajamas and toilet kit and went out to change in the bathroom. That was a mistake. There was no toilet seat, only a hole in the floor. Around it was what previous passengers had left. Their aim had not been very good. All the holes of all the bathrooms in the whole train were connected by a slow-moving flow of water. So while you were doing your business, you were totally aware of what the rest of the train's bathroom visitors were doing. The stench was overpowering.

I returned to my compartment, only to find my companions sound asleep in their beds, supposedly in their pajamas.

I later learned that I could very well have undressed in their presence. Nudity does not have the same sexual connotations among Asians as among Caucasians.

Now it was morning, and I had just finished reading Pearl Buck's *The Good Earth*. Reading this wonderful book while the train was passing through China's rice fields, villages and hills, so well described by the author, was a lovely experience.

Chinese Customs

Finding newspapers or magazines in English or in any other language except Chinese was extremely difficult, and my "ten useful Chinese phrases" were woefully inadequate for Chinese newsprint. But the day before in Shanghai I had managed to buy both a New York Herald Tribune and a Time Magazine. I felt rich and was savoring the moment when I would start reading them. They would be carefully rationed to last during many lonely evenings in Chinese hotel rooms. I still had two weeks travel left.

The train stopped at a station whose name I couldn't read. A young lady boarded the train, and sat down in my compartment. I smiled at her and she smiled back. An hour passed, and I had a feeling, that she would like to talk with me. I too, wanted very much to talk with her, but with no more than ten phrases to my disposal, that was impossible. Finally she took a deep breath and said to my great surprise and delight, "May I speak English to you?"

When I answered," Of course, with pleasure", she said,

"You see, I am on my way to take an interpreter examination and I really need to practice speaking English. I have never spoken English with a Caucasian and have never read anything that was originally written in English, only translated. I would give anything to have a chance to read an English or American newspaper!"

I was tempted to just listen politely and nod understandingly. However, I gave her The Herald Tribune; Time I kept for myself.

When I arrived in Guilin, a young lady, who knew my name and said she had been sent to take me to the "Hotel for Foreigners," picked me up at the train station. At least that is what I understood. She spoke very little English, and was wearing some kind of uniform. We couldn't communicate much and, to this day, I don't know who sent her and how she knew my name. The authorities? An-Fu? The guards who had checked me on the train?

This was in the early eighties and foreigners were a curiosity, especially in the countryside. I found, that wherever I walked, people gathered around to look at my feet. First, I thought that they looked at my sandals. But then I realized my *toes* were the objects of their curiosity. They had never seen red toenails and were fascinated by them.

I thought this a good moment to take photographs of them. It was obvious they didn't like that at all. But when they found to their great surprise that the pictures came out of the camera right away, they were amazed. I took as many pictures as I could, especially of the children, and handed them to their mothers. My Polaroid (and I!) were a great hit.

The "Hotel for Foreigners" was all right, but I didn't want to be surrounded by foreigners in China, so I ventured out on my own. I walked into a small restaurant in the neighborhood and sat down. No waiter paid any attention to me. After about half an hour I left. Later I was told that it wasn't that they were rude; they just knew that they couldn't understand me, and that meant loosing face. So ignoring me was the best solution. For them!

I went back to the hotel, had my dinner there and arranged for a cruise on the river Li.

That cruise was a lovely experience. On both sides of the river were those pointed mountaintops, interspersed with red and golden temples. Our boat wended its way between rafts and houseboats of all kinds, with people fishing, washing clothes, cooking and eating, obviously spending their whole lives on the river. Theirs was a life totally different from anything I had ever seen. Later in Hong Kong, I found a large area called Aberdeen where people have lived on their houseboats for generations.

My friend Marge and I traveled to all the interesting places in and around Beijing: The Forbidden City, The Emperors' Tombs and The Great Wall. Walking on this great monument, the only human construction, which at that time could be seen from the moon, alone, with only a friend, no crowds, tour buses nor hawkers, is something I shall always remember.

When I first arrived in China, directly from the U.S., I had to list all those of my possessions, which were difficult to buy in China. This was to prevent them from being sold on the black market. So I listed my cameras, jewelry, watches and also my tape recorder. Now I was leaving, and at customs in Canton there was an officer in military uniform, armed with a pistol, who checked people's lists, as they were passing through. Only *now* did I remember the tape recorder I had given to An-Fu.

I broke out in a cold sweat. What would happen to me? My explanation that I had given it to a father so that he could listen to his children's voices, I didn't think would impress the uniformed customs officer. He would say, "You have broken the law, and for that you go to jail in China." But for some reason he didn't notice that the tape recorder was missing from my luggage. With a sigh of relief I continued on my way to Hong Kong.

An-Fu is now happily re-united with Victoria and their children and grandchildren. And, I have bought a new tape recorder.

36

The Perfect Gift

On my calendar for December my daughter Katya had written:

"Buy *big* Christmas gift for Katya."

I saw her note so I told her, "So you want a *big* Christmas present? I had thought of a *small* one, you know, the kind that comes in a little square box."

"Oh," she said, "I'd like that even more!"

So, some time before Christmas I looked through my jewelry box. In the past I had given her many beautiful pieces of jewelry, which I had been given by my mother or inherited from my grandmother. Katya was always very pleased to get them, as was I, when I saw her wearing jewelry, which I remember my mother wearing.

Alas, my jewelry box was almost empty of things I wasn't wearing myself. But then I saw in the corner a little Chinese box. I opened it and there was a beautiful jade pendant—a lovely green circle about the size of a half-dollar, encircled in gold and with a beautiful gold Chinese symbol on each side. I had totally forgotten I had it, but I remembered now, that I had bought it in a funny little shop in Beijing, in 1984. I recalled my friend Marge telling me, that you must always bargain in China, or they will loose respect for you. Bargaining is difficult when you only know ten phrases, but I managed to get the pendant, for what I thought was a reasonable price.

I took it to my favorite jeweler to evaluate. He appraised it as, "very good." So, I had the perfect Christmas gift for my daughter.

Before wrapping it the night before Christmas I saw it was time to get ready for my dinner date with Bob, so on impulse I put it on. It looked absolutely stunning with what I was wearing!

During dinner Bob said, "What a beautiful necklace! I have never seen it before. When did you get it?" I told him I had kept it for many years but never worn it.

"Well, you should wear it more often. It looks great, especially with that dress."

We went to a concert after dinner, where no less than three people complimented me on my beautiful necklace! Now I wanted to keep it for myself! But I didn't. I gave it to my daughter for Christmas. When she opened it, she burst out, "Oh, Mama, thank you! I always hoped that one day you would give this to me!" I was totally perplexed.

"How did you know I had it? I have never worn it. In fact, I had completely forgotten about it myself!"

"Oh," she said, "a long time ago, when you said I could borrow your pearl bracelet, I saw the little box, and couldn't resist opening it."

A couple of days later I asked a Chinese friend of mine, what the two symbols mean. One signifies love and the other unselfishness.

37

I Saved the Best for Last

"You have had such a wonderful life," said a friend the other day, after hearing about my adventures around the world.

"What do you mean 'have had?' I asked. "I'm not dead yet! I'm still having a wonderful life."

And I have found a man, one I think I'll keep. His name is Bob, and we met at a tennis tournament in La Jolla, California, twenty-five years ago. He was team captain and drew my name out of a hat. Our team won. I liked him right away, especially when he said, "We won thanks to you!"

Bob is good-looking, sun-tanned and very fit. He plays tennis four times a week and swims three. His hair is black; at least it was when we first met. He likes to eat in good restaurants, which is great, since I don't like to cook. When I found out that his company sends him (and a companion) on business trips all over the world, and he found out that I had a tennis court, we liked each other even more!

Bob takes me on cruises all over the world: from *Ushuaia*, the world's south-ern-most town, to Spits Bergen, near the North Pole, on the Yangtze River, the Black Sea, The South Pacific and Australia. We always get a cabin with a balcony and sometimes with our own butler. We love the same things: ballroom dancing, swimming and, of course, tennis.

Most importantly, we love each other.

I think Aunt Elsa would approve of Bob and think I made a good choice!

So am I going to marry him? Not on your life! That would ruin everything. The idea of having a man around twenty-four/seven is not my idea of enjoying life! No, we live together Thursday evening through Sunday. That way I only have to prepare his breakfast three times a week, and I never have to wash his socks!

"But, if you marry him, you'll always have him to help you around the house," said one of my friends.

With My "POSSLQ"

"I would? Don't bet on it! He is no good around the house (except in the bed-room!)"

He has, as the Swedes say, "*tummen mitt i handen,*" (his thumb in the middle of his hand) meaning totally useless with his hands. Once, when he put artichoke leaves in the garbage disposal, (which I had told him not to do) he tried to repair the damage by pouring chlorine into it. The metal blades disintegrated.

When I asked him to put up a sign of the name of my house, he broke not only the sign, but the hammer as well.

And when he put together the garbage can cart, he put the handles on back-wards.

The other day I asked him to put in a light bulb. How he did it I don't know, but the light didn't work. How many financial advisors do you *need* to screw in a light bulb?

When I tell our friends about it, Bob says he does it purposely, so I won't ask him for help any more. Well, true or not, he got his wish. I don't ask him any more.

There is just one small problem with our relationship. When Bob introduces me, he says, "I'd like you to meet my lady." Very nice; I like that.

But what am I supposed to say? "I'd like you to meet my *lord*?"

I suppose I could say my *significant other* or my main *squeeze*. And then there is my *POSSL Q*, an IRS acronym meaning "Persons of Opposite Sex Sharing Living Quarters."

But that is a minor problem. I learned one thing traveling around the world; having a man Thursday through Sunday is enough, at least for this Swedish girl.

I think Aunt Elsa would approve of that, too.

978-0-595-45373-3
0-595-45373-2